Freeing the West

Freeing the West

◆

A Path to Truth, Justice and Equality

Wajid Mahmud Ibn Bashir

iUniverse, Inc.
New York Lincoln Shanghai

Freeing the West
A Path to Truth, Justice and Equality

iUniverse books may be ordered through booksellers or by contacting:

iUniverse
2021 Pine Lake Road, Suite 100
Lincoln, NE 68512
www.iuniverse.com
1-800-Authors (1-800-288-4677)

ISBN-13: 978-0-595-35143-5 (pbk)
ISBN-13: 978-0-595-79845-2 (ebk)
ISBN-10: 0-595-35143-3 (pbk)
ISBN-10: 0-595-79845-4 (ebk)

Printed in the United States of America

"In the name of Allah, the Gracious, the Merciful.
Praise be to Allah, the Lord of the worlds,
The Gracious, the Merciful.
Master of the Day of Judgment.
Thee do we serve and Thee do we ask for help.
Guide us on the right path,
The path of those upon whom Thou hast bestowed favors,
Not those upon whom wrath is brought down, nor those who go astray." (1:1-7)
The Holy Qur'an

"Freedom is a prerogative of all living things, man being no exception. Liberty is the most cherished fruit of life. Man is the epitome of liberty which is ingrained in him. His very texture is woven with the yarns of liberty. Yet, amazingly, we find all man-made institutions shaped to work against the liberty of man in the final analysis." Hadhrat Mirza Tahir Ahmad, Fourth Khalifa of the Ahmadiyya Movement in Islam

Contents

AUTHOR'S NOTE

After the Thirteen colonies were established a new world for the Europeans was formed. The Constitution that was written by the early leaders of the United States enabled every free man to seek out the newborn American dream and to seek out his own freedom. This dream was conceived when all of the dreamers were of one color, White.

As the Thirteen colonies grew into fifty states the population of the Americans decreased and the amount of enslaved Africans grew yet the "American Dream" still only existed in the minds of White free males. Where was this same dream for men or women of the other colors of the rainbow? Would George Washington in his wildest imagination imagine a man from Brazil owning a house next-door to him? Today, that Brazilian is right next-door. Was the constitution designed to fit the needs of this Brazilian? Was the Constitution even designed to fit the ever changing needs of the White man himself?

The Constitution has been changed and reformed many times to fit the ever growing needs of man as he evolves socially and mentally. All of these changes were man made. Yet as long as man is prone to mistakes, will there ever be a code of reason and living that will desire no change but still be able to guide mankind together to live in harmony?

The financial wealth of the European countries helped the concept of idolatry to emerge into its next stage of life here on North American soil. This concept was designed to give every free man a chance at a decent living and economic growth. Just like socialism, capitalism was also designed to replace religion and morality. The search for financial gain became the way out for man of all his social problems and helped economy and government replaced the laws of God. But will the constant paper chase ensure the survival of mankind's species? Will his greed for wealth and power only force him to revert back to his lower animal instincts of survival of the strongest? Ultimately squashing beneath his feet all those whose income quota is not high enough to stand up and be noticed.

Religion is one's way of life through condoning, regulating, and motivating one's actions and thoughts. It is a way of life that one can accept through conversion or birth. Just like installing a new program into a computer the computer of the mind becomes saturated with the new program and begins to distribute the new information to the main components of the body, the heart, the limbs, the brain and the tongue.

After a complete download, this new program begins to be visible in the person's actions, thoughts, and speech transforming him into a new person. When fully downloaded this new person will have changed his way of thought and action according to the new programs defined regulations thus making the person's immediate environment a different place. As the program spreads it will begin to change the person, his family, his city, his state and ultimately the world.

The purpose of religion is meant to create an environment where all mankind can exist together unified under one code of ethics leading them towards moral, physical and spiritual unity. If one driver is doing 35 in a 35mph zone and the other is doing 80 an accident is bound to happen. The same occurs in religion. If one way of life is causing one believer to think one way and the other believer is living totally opposite accidents and conflicts are bound to happen.

The only way the two people will be able to coexist side by side is if they find a belief system designed to keep them both up to the same speed. True Islam is that way of life. True Islam is the only way of life given to all men till the end of time whether White, Black, Red, Yellow, or Brown. We have seen the fall of many great empires and we are now witnessing the fall of capitalism. The only way of life that will exist in the end is True Islam.

The destiny of the Western people lies in Islam. Your history has exhausted all other available options. If you examine your history you will see that the existence of the worship of false helpless idols has been present since the birth of your people. You have been poisoned with this overpowering doctrine since the earliest of times yet over and over you have allowed this false doctrine to destroy and cripple your people.

Your people have traveled across the globe to escape the plague that the worship of false gods brings with it. There is nowhere else to go. The time is now that the Western people must stand up for their survival and cast down the yoke of your false gods or it will only lead to torment. True Islam is the only insurance policy that is available to give the Western people the knowledge it needs to save itself in these trying times.

Just a note of clarification: whenever I have mentioned the Holy Prophet Mohammad (saw), you will see "(saw)" after the mention. This notation is short for "Sallalaho alaihe wa salaam" which means "Peace and blessings of Allah be on him." This is a blessing and prayer that said every time his name is mentioned.

WHY RELIGION?

○ ○

In the Name of Allah the Gracious, Ever Merciful.

All men must die and be brought before God. At the point of death you will sub-mit to the will of God by sighing your last breath. The question is not whether you call yourself a Muslim or not, but whether you choose to live a Muslim way of life. Many faiths put so much focus on death because they offer no way of helping its followers here in the physical world. They offer no solutions to the everyday problems that man is forced to endure while living his term on earth. The half emptiness of these idolatrous beliefs leave the cup of prosperity only half full while Islam offers mankind a full cup to quench his thirst and lead him to happiness and comfort in this life as well as the next.

We hear of "scholars of Islam" but what makes a scholar a scholar? Just because you went to an Islamic school does that make everything you know and say right? If you learned your entire life that 2+2=5, does that mean you are right? In order for you to be a scholar, you must be able to prove that your information produces true and correct results. If knowing information is the only requirement to be a scholar how do we determine if the scholar is one of truth or ignorance? Every human must do his own homework to find if the information he is being taught is true or false. Would you buy a car without researching its history? Buy-ing a car is a major investment yet it is nowhere as important as your way of life. Never the less people take less time to research their beliefs and way of life than they do when buying a car. If you wouldn't let someone else buy you a car than why leave the safety of your future in someone else's grasp.

Religion is like mathematics. As mankind evolved mentally he was taught the basics of addition, subtraction, division, and multiplication. After each nation had learned its own "mathematical concept" God decided that man had evolved enough to move on to "algebra" and to all be taught the same thing in a com-bined perfected form. Islam is the "calculus" of the religious world because it is all the schools of faith perfected into one all encompassing equation for all of the nations of the world and for all of time. In school, you continue learning more and more usages of addition and subtraction so why wouldn't God continue to advance mankind's moral training as mankind evolved mentally. The need for man to continue learning is what drives us to be better in all areas of life with religion being no different. Muhammad (saw) was not the founder of Islam since God Himself perfected the faith. God was the founder who perfected this way of life. Muhammad (saw) was a mortal whom God used as an example to show how Islam was to be put into affect in our daily lives. In the Qur'an God says He has perfected a faith for man and He has called it Islam. If something is perfected that means it existed before, so if the ways of Islam existed under some other name before Muhammad (saw) then how could he have founded it? People often say that Islam copied many of its tenants from other faiths but is the word copy suitable to use?

The One True God that revealed all the revelations to man is the same One True God so does it make sense that God would reveal opposing guidelines to different peoples? The guidelines He revealed were for the purpose of all men to live together. Islam is the perfection of all of God's teachings for the benefit of all men. The Arabic word for religion is defined in English as "a way of life." A way of life governs your way of thinking and the actions you commit. A person who thinks good thoughts usually commits good actions. Politics is an action that must be governed by a thought so it is also governed by your way of life. Morality and politics cannot be separated because if a person is a moral person he will be a moral politician yet if a person is immoral he will be an immoral politician. The influence of his moral upbringing will never be taken out and will always show in the decisions he makes in the political arena by the actions he chooses to make. So why do we have the separation of church and state in the United States?

At the time the United States was being formed, the church had a tight grip on the ruling class of the European countries. The new settlers knew that if they were to take full advantage of the newly conquered lands the tenants of the church would hold them back. Although the church represented morality and righteousness, the newly formed country was in no way going to bow down to the laws of the church. True Islam does not teach physical revolution against the government or ruling body in any way yet gives man the guidance to be able to exist within any form of government. The newly formed states had seen the mistakes made by the church in Europe and told themselves they would not let them happen here. The Qur'an made this same law 1,500 years ago when it gave man the right to choose his own beliefs. In Europe at that time a person's faith was determined by what his king was and to choose differently was often punishable by death. This was a fact that many Europeans had a problem with because of the many differences in opinions, laws, and tribes.

The Period of Reformation and Enlightenment in Europe occurred for the purpose of physical, religious, and political change. Sects were started only because group of men want to satisfy their own personal desires even if they went against the will of the original message. If a true message revealed by God Himself becomes infected with the ignorance of man, then it is no longer a revealed religion but a distorted mutation. Once distorted will the message produce the same effect on humanity the original message was intended to bring about? Does true morality and faith need to be changed? Has God changed His laws? If not, why would God appoint weak men to change them for Him? Would God make a change so drastic that it would be totally opposite from what He said before? Only man would make a change like that since man is not perfect. Can these changes still produce the same response as the original message?

Absolute submission to the will of God: What could be better or bring mankind closer to his Creator? What more could a man desire? Not the will of a man or the will of a government. The will of God should be the only thing man should yearn for all his life. Conform to God's wishes and all of man's needs will be met and fulfilled. God is a Merciful and Forgiving God. If He wanted all of us to be the same He could have done that but He has decided to make us different to test us to see if we are worthy of receiving the many rewards He has to offer.

A Muslim is submissive to the will of the One True God. God says to be humble and not excessive in thought or action. Superiority is excessive pride in ones self, tribe, property, or ethnicity. Any action displaying this emotion leads one farther away from the hands of God and the blessings He offers the humble.

All men of the world have had their fair share of wisdom whether physical or mental thus making their fair share of advancements in the fields of science, politics, medicine, and agriculture. Do these advancements make one man better than another or give one man the right of ownership over another's way of life and thought? Does one man's financial and military prowess give him the right to control and dictate another man's action? The Western nations have made such articles as the Bill of Rights and the Constitution so these rights of freedom should also extend to men of other nations as well as the inhabitants of its own. Every man should have the freedom to make his own choices and be responsible for his own thoughts and actions.

If a Muslim adopts Christian ways, he is no longer a Muslim. Similarly, if a Christian adopts Muslim ways he is no longer a Christian. The debate is not whether to adopt the others ways but rather to convert to the other faith and way of life. First you must examine the faith to find out if the faith will give you the responses you are searching for. Will the faith bring you closer to God and the truth He offers? Will your faith bring you closer to other men and the things God has created for the comfort of man? Will the faith you practice bring you closer to the knowledge of this world and the next? Will the faith ensure your mental, financial, and physical safety? These are the questions anyone searching for a way of life should ask himself about the perspective faith. Muslims should question their faith as well as Christians in order to get as much knowledge as possible.

The moral function of a religious faith is to separate a creative energy from a destructive energy. Islam is a pro-active versus a re-active religion. Islam warns of and discourages an act even before it is committed because God knows what the response from that act will be. Would you warn your child not to touch the open flame even when curiosity is a natural instinct of a young child? This is done only for the protection of the child both mentally and physically. God has given us instructions how to protect us from inflicting harm on others and ourselves. In Islam there is no priesthood because the belief that man needs a physical interme-diary between man and God is non-existent. On the mental level this need does not exist because every single man is equipped to have one on one communica-tion with God if his heart and mind is open. On the physical level it allows each man the right to learn the scriptures and writings of his faith on his own, through education to learn, to read, and to write. Education is foremost in Islam because without being able to read for one's self how can the faith truly be learned? Lis-tening to someone else forces you to become enslaved to the teacher and not to the lesson being taught. Education also allows the practitioner to become free to learn on his own and to be able to question others about the faith ultimately get-ting away from blind faith.

Without the proper moral and spiritual guidance man will never be able to suppress and control the lower animal urges that dwell within. One of the instincts that exist within the animal nature is the marking of territories. Animals are constantly trying to enlarge their territories through fighting. To think that mankind is any different is illogical. Whether this territorial power trip is through finance, military might, education, or political power it all stems from the lower urges of greed we all know inhabit our being. This is where guidance from God comes into play. He helps us to control these urges leading us towards a life of unity and fairness with each other no matter of ethnicity, economic status, sex, or age. The hateful attitude that exist between the Eastern and Western portions of the globe exist because somewhere along the line mankind stopped trying to advance itself spiritually and morally thus allowing the evil desires to monopolize the time in the minds of the inhabitants of both sides. It doesn't matter which side is richer or whose military is stronger because neither side has been able to resist its own lower impulses.

When a parent gives an order does he or she wish that order to remain in affect till he or she decides it is time to be changed? What if the son or daughter decides to just change the wishes of the parent without the proper authorization? Would the parent be angered and respond with disappointment and punishment? The parent knows what is best for the child so if a command is given it is usually in the best interest and safety of the child. So why should a commandment of God need changed especially if God knows the future? Do you think He would put a commandment in His scriptures that would require change by a weak man?

The West, even if not physically engaged in war against its neighbors, has definitely inspired feelings of anger and resentment in many parts of the globe through the usage of discrimination, hatred, and over-excessive pride. By calling itself the most civilized nation on the earth it instantly degrades the other nations as being lesser in status financially, morally, and mentally. By saying that it is the South American countries that have addicted Americans to cocaine makes them the enemy in the war against drugs. By saying that AIDS came from Africa causes anger against that particular region and so on and so on. The Western nations have developed different stereotypes for nearly every ethnicity of people inside and outside their borders which are only meant to cause hatred and repulsion.

One can receive a commandment but that does not mean he will follow it. If the follower does not follow the command does it mean the command is wrong or the follower is wrong? If a parent tells a child not to commit an act and the child disobeys does that make the parent wrong or responsible? That is what has happened to so many religious faiths over the course of time with Islam being no different. Men through their own weakness and greed have defined the commands of God to fit their own personal desires even if they go completely against the will of God Himself. Although many changes have been made the True Islam still remains strong under the protection of God.

Can the forces of the West stop Islam or Muslims? Islam is truth, freedom, and peace. As long as mankind is in search of these values the road they take will only and always lead them to the beauty of True Islam. Superiority can be defined in many ways such as financial, military, religious, or technological. What does Islam say makes one superior over others? Righteousness. In the eyes of God this is the only thing that makes a man great. What are the characteristics of righteousness? Truthfulness. Humbleness. Helpfulness. Cleanliness. And the list goes on and on. Only when a man becomes as righteous as possible will he be considered *"the best of you"* in the eyes of the One who is the final judge.

An expert must know the truth and be willing to prove it as the truth. A man can only say he is an expert when he has learned all the correct information about a certain object. Only the author of a book can be an expert about it because no one else can know everything about the book and exactly what the book means except the author. The Qur'an is no different. Men can claim to understand its verses but the only one who will ever be able to understand its complete meaning is its author, God. We can only do our best with our limited knowledge to understand the information God wishes us to understand.

Some experts in the West say Islamic ideas lead to terrorism. If the idea leads to terror than the idea must be a terrible idea. An idea that is bad will only brings bad actions. This is found true by retracing the steps that led up to the action being committed. Let's retrace one of the most celebrated acts in U.S. history, the Boston Tea Party.

1. King ruled government

2. The King made the taxes

3. Taxes were enforced by the government

4. The colonies were angered they had to pay taxes

5. The Tea was dumped in the ocean

The act of defiance in dumping the tea in the ocean was towards the political control the King had over the colonies. Terrorism is a reaction being displayed by a physical act of aggression. When you examine the history of the world and all the acts of terrorism that have occurred throughout the globe you will question yourself as to why religion is blamed when it comes to terrorism in the Middle East? Islam was the last revealed religion so what religious ideology contributed to the many acts of terrorism committed before its existence? Religion is an easier scapegoat than politics because politics can be proven wrong beyond a shadow of a doubt while the argument of religion goes on forever thus leaving the true culprit free to wreck havoc.

Men can say many things about the religion of Islam but why say anything at all? What is it about Islam that causes so much hatred? It is the spiritual, moral, and physical freedom that Islam ensures. This is where the West has gone wrong. They say that other countries hate America because of its freedom but in reality the Western leaders are doing everything they can to keep Western minds off of the true freedoms that exist within Islam. Throughout history men have used more than just chains to enslave others with the West being no different. The serfs that lived under the rule of the European kings often lived in extreme poverty forcing their everyday existence to be one of hardship and strife. This physical slavery has been replaced by a mental bondage causing even worse results in the nature of the West.

There are many reasons why the West is being held back from the beauty of Islam, but I have chosen not to go into detail at this time. However I ensure you that the reward of Islam is the true reward that your people have been searching for for thousands of years. Haven't you found it strange that those in West are one of the last peoples to see the beauty and truth of Islam? The West believes that their way of life is superior to all others but if it is truly superior then why so much fear when it comes to Islam? What is it about the Islamic way of life that causes Western people to cringe with fear and hatred at the mention of this humble way of life? Is it the ignorant acts that have been perpetrated in the name of Islam? Is it the cultural habits of the Middle East that have Western people filled with hatred? What Western people do not understand is that Islam is the truth for them also. Islam is the dream they thought they could find here in North America. It is not where you are or who you are it is what you are. Western people are taught to fear and hate the one thing that they are looking for, freedom. Islam is the freedom that Western people have been searching for thousands of years yet they continue to be blinded by ignorance, greed, and hatred. Islam is the only way that will bring about the changes the Western world desires such as justice, peace, and freedom.

Islam through the wisdom its Creator offers countless human rights. God stated in His book the Qur'an that He has sent messengers to every people on the face of the earth with each messenger recognizing the fact that his message was meant for the tribe to which he was sent. Each messenger received revelation that was strictly meant to handle the needs and problems of a specific group of people. Muhammad (saw) is the only messenger to make the claim that his message was sent for the entire world. What does this mean? The message of Muhammad (saw) was meant to satisfy the needs, requirements, and problems of mankind as one people. This was the only time God had sent a messenger to the entire human civilization. This was done because the message of Islam is meant to bring together the different ethnicities and cultures under one code of ethics. Islam is meant to unite the people of the world under worshipping the One True God and to bring freedom to all mankind. True Islam is the only way of life that safeguards the ways and rights of all humans since it is the only faith sent for the reformation of all men. It singles out no certain group or tribe of people only dividing the believers from the non-believers. It does not separate or elevate the rights of Whites over Blacks or Blacks over Whites. It gives all men an equal playing field in the eyes of God since the ultimate goal of mankind is the pleasure of God, as He simply states in His revealed book:

"Whoso acts righteously, whether male or female and is a believer, We will surely grant him a pure life; and We will surely bestow on such their reward according to the best of their works." (16:97).

The Qur'an offers a reply to the statements made by numerous Western authors that Islam says women have no souls. The promise of God Almighty is twofold. In that the doers of good both men and women that lead a good life in this world will have a reward in the next life. It can't get put any simpler. God is promising all individuals that if they do right and worship Him He will grant them happiness. So if a man cannot find peace it must be something man is doing on his own. Each one of us is responsible for his own life. Islam teaches man to respect and protect the rights of all creatures whether male or female, living or non-living. Islam states that God offers rewards to all who obey His commandments.

The leaders of the Western community wonder of the future of the West. The future of the Western world will only be a reflection of its treatment of the rest of the world. All the actions that it has done to the rest of the world will come back to haunt them and only by turning to the way of life that God has laid out for them will they be able to avoid the reaction of their bad actions. I hope this book will help the West to understand this way of life and lead them closer to the true freedom and peace for which they have been searching. Islam is a way of life that is protected by God Himself so to think that a weak man with his weak weapons can ever overcome the Creator of the Heavens and Earth is mere lunacy. The truth of Islam will exist till the end of time in all four corners of the globe.

"Those who dispute about the messages of Allah without any authority having come to them, there is naught in their breasts but (desire) to become great, which they will never attain. So seek refuge in Allah. Surely He is the Hearing, the Seeing." (40:56).

This is the only message needed to be given to the West. The need for me to write this book is only that the people of the Western world may be given the correct information so that the rewards of God may be placed upon them and that the burden of falsehood will be removed. I pray that this book will bring people of the West closer to the freedom and peace all men wish to attain.

QUR'AN AND WAR

What is the fear of Islam in the hearts and minds of those in the West based on? Ignorance and lack of knowledge caused by men of ignorance. If God wanted to cause fear and destruction do you think He would use weak men since He is the same God who created the Heavens and the Earth from nothing. Only a fool believes that weak men are the tools of God's wrath.

The Western nations respect power whether it is military, financial, educational, or spiritual. Power is all the Western people have ever known from the time of the Caesars to the time of today. The only thing that has made the Western people known in the community of the world is its power. The people of the West have never been known for their love of education, morality or spirituality but only for their love of power. It is this brainwashing effect of false power that has poisoned the Western people causing them to be blinded from the truth that the only true power exists in the One True God. This brainwashing led the Caesars to expand their empire over two thirds of the then known world. This brainwashing led the Europeans to wipe out Americans. This brainwashing caused the atomic bomb to be dropped on Japan resulting in the death of hundreds of thousands of innocent men, women and children. This brainwashing is the reason farmers get paid not to grow crops while millions starve in Africa.

It's the delusion that one has the power to play God. But Christianity has told us God is a White man hanging on a cross, so why shouldn't this same man have the power to determine who lives and who dies? This is the same man who fed the early Christians to the lions and burned the "witches" of Salem while they were alive. This is not intended to be a bashing ceremony but only a way of showing that the only true way to respect power is to worship the All Powerful One who makes no mistakes. Islam teaches respect on every level. Respect from parent to child and child to parent. Respect from civilian to government and government to civilian. Respect from country to country. Respect from man to animal, man to nature, and ultimately from man to God. Islam leaves no stone unturned on the topic of relationships between man and his surroundings. The Prophet Muhammad (saw) is the model given to mankind to teach how to use Islam to deal with other humans and non-humans. The episodes that occurred in his life have given mankind the information on the proper way of dealing with all aspects of human and non-human relations. Islam teaches one to be respectful of the rights of others and how to correct actions of disrespect.

What is the need for religion in such a "modern" age? Man has thought that the need for organized religion was a waste of time with prayer, and fasting, only a burden. Why praise a God that was never seen when the greatness of man is witnessed every day. Yet has the greatness of man done anything for mankind? Islam is the final frontier for mankind. It is the last and greatest step in the evolution of the human species. Most of the West sees itself as all-powerful, but this isn't the case. Only through this true religion will mankind save himself from extinction and annihilation. Only through morality will man cease from regressing back to his lower animalistic self. Only through faith in the One True God will mankind find the guidelines to preservation and freedom.

All the false idols man has created over the centuries will give him nothing but despair, hopelessness, and misguidance. Within a true religion man will not only find the middle path that will lead him to the heavens of the next world, but also create a heaven in the present world. No matter what his proud mind may think man does not posses the knowledge to secure his freedom. Only the pure guidance of the Almighty can complete such a job. A religion that has the pure teachings from God can fulfill the needs of men. This religion must be able to offer all the methods of treatment our diseased world begs for. Through total submission to the will of God mankind will dig itself out of the pit of despair he has allowed himself to be swallowed by. Islam is that shovel which mankind must use to free itself from disaster.

Public opinion is based on the knowledge the public has of a certain subject. If you grew up all your life and everybody you knew told you that apples were foul to the taste you would grow up thinking they were disgusting even though you never had one. The more people that told you apples were not good the more you would believe them because there is no way all those people could be wrong. Then one day you saw a person throwing up while holding an apple. You would immediately assume it was because of the apple that he was vomiting.

This is exactly what has happened to Islam. You've heard rumors and stories. Everybody has told you such terrible things about this way of life. You've even seen Muslims committing horrible acts and all the while you still think it is all because of Islam.

Well, all of that has led you here to discover what it is about Islam that has put such a bad taste in people's mouth in the West. What is it about this way of life that claims to be all about peace yet you see so much violence committed by its followers? Don't let public opinion turn into public enslavement. Don't let what I say in this book make up your mind for you. Continue reading this book and doing other research with true information and I guarantee that falsehood will be shattered by truth. Don't allow your opinion to be controlled by outside forces and influence. Only by researching the truth can you form your own opinion. Free your mind from public opinion and seek the truth for which you yearn.

Many Westerners wonder who speaks for Islam. God speaks for Islam. The Qur'an is the revealed word of God. The Qur'an enables man to understand the reason why God has created mankind. In order for mankind to be able to follow His guidebook God gave us Prophets to be examples of the laws that He revealed. These Prophets were given revelation so that we could understand the beauty of God and to show us that His revealed word could be utilized and performed in our everyday lives. The Prophets were sent so that weak people like ourselves could have a model for us to fashion our behavior after in order to lead us closer to the success of God's playbook.

Often the ignorance of the Western writers is shown when they discuss the verses pertaining to fighting in the Qur'an. During the early days of Islam the Muslims were under extreme persecution from the idolatrous Meccans. The Meccans tried their hardest to exterminate the faith of the One True God by killing the Muslims. Kill the follower and the message will die also. God knew this and after seeing how his followers endured torture for many years He gave the Prophet permission to fight in defense of the faith. This permission to fight was given only for the survival of the faith. Freedom from religious persecution is the only reason to go to war and even then are the situations governed with extreme caution.

A call to war for Muslims can only be given if the following requirements are met:

1. War is to be resorted to only for the sake of God and not for the sake of any selfish motives, not for the aggrandizement or for the advancement of any other interest.

2. Muslims can go to war only against one who attacks them first.

3. Muslims can fight only those who fight against them. They cannot fight against those who take no part in warfare.

4. Even if the enemy has initiated the attack, it is our duty to keep warfare within limits. To extend the war, either territorially or in respect of weapons used, is wrong.

5. Muslims are only to fight only a regular army charged by the enemy to fight on his side. Muslims are not to fight others on the enemies' side.

6. In warfare immunity is to be afforded to all religious rites and observances. If the enemy spares the places where religious ceremonies are held, then Muslims must desist from fighting in such places.

7. If the enemy uses a place of worship as a base of attack, then Muslims may return attack. If not being used for bases of attack to destroy religious places is extremely forbidden.

8. If the enemy realizes the danger and the mistake of using a religious place as a base, and changes the battlefront, then Muslims must conform to the change. The fact that the enemy started the attack from a religious place is not to be used as an excuse for attacking the religious place.

9. Fighting is to continue only so long as interference with religion and religious freedom lasts. When religion becomes free and interference with it is no longer permitted and the enemy declares and begins to act accordingly, then there is to be no war, even if it is the enemy who starts it.

These laws of Islam concerning war and fighting clearly state that the usage of suicide bombing and other forms of terrorism are completely un-Islamic and prohibited by God, Almighty. To call an act an act of terrorism "Islamic" is completely incorrect and a lie. Wars have been forced upon Muslims but if the enemy desists it is the duty of Muslims to desist also and forgive the past. When the enemy does not desist and attacks Muslims again and again then he should remember the fate of the earlier Prophets. Muslims are to fight while religious persecution lasts but when the aggressor stops so must the Muslims. Muslims have no right to meddle with another people's religion even if that religion seems to be false. All the battles fought by the Prophet Muhammad (saw) and the Muslims were because they were the victims of unprovoked aggression. The enemies of Islam had chosen to disturb the peace of the Muslims and the territory around them. To retaliate against such unprovoked aggression seems natural, just, and necessary. True Muslims must stop fighting as soon as the enemy stops. All that the enemy is required to concede is freedom of belief and worship.

Muslims in the course of battle must incline to peace with the disbelievers if at any time it is offered even at the risk of being deceived. Muslims are to put their trust in God thus cheating will never avail against Muslims who rely on the help of God. Their victories are due not to themselves but to God. Even in the darkest and most difficult of times God has stood by the Prophet and his true followers. When Muslims go out to war they are to make sure that the unreasonableness of war has been explained to the enemy and that he still wants war. If Muslims turn down proposals of peace they will not be fighting for God but for self-aggrandizement and worldly gain. Killing is not the aim of war since the one whom we wish to kill today may be guided tomorrow. Could Muslims have become Muslims if they had not been spared? Muslims are to abstain from mass killing because lives spared may turn out to be lives guided towards righteousness. God is well aware of what men do and to what ends and with what motives they do it whether Muslim or non-Muslim.

It is forbidden that Muslims should make prisoners of his enemy except during times of war involving much bloodshed. The system of making prisoners of enemy tribes without war and bloodshed was practiced until and even after the advent of Islam. Slavery is strongly prohibited in Islam. Even rules of treatment towards prisoners are detailed in the Qur'an. According to Islam the best thing is to let prisoners go without asking for ransom. As this is not always possible, release for ransom is also provided for. Muslim teachings do not only consist of precepts laid down in the Qur'an but also include the examples of the Prophet who was the living practicing embodiment of the Qur'an. The following are the sayings of the Prophet on the subject of war.

1. Muslims are forbidden to mutilate the dead.

2. Muslims are forbidden to cheat in war.

3. Children and women are not to be killed.

4. Priests and religious leaders are not to be interfered with.

5. Old men and women are not to be killed.

6. When Muslims enter a territory, they should not strike fear into the general population. They should permit no ill treatment of the common folk.

7. A Muslim army should not camp where it causes inconvenience to the general public. It should not block roads used by wayfarers.

8. No disfigurement of faces is permitted.

9. The least possible losses should be inflicted on the enemy.

10. Prisoners of war who are related should be kept together.

11. Muslims should care more for the comfort of their prisoners than of their own.

12. Delegates from other countries should be held in great respect.

The Prophet of Allah (saw) was so insistent on these rules for a fighting army he declared that whoever did not observe these rules, would not fight for God but for his own self. The next time you hear of a so called Islamic act of terrorism see if it violates any of these rules and if it does, it was not condoned by a Islam but by one who is greedy for the false wealth of this physical world.

Muhammad (saw) fought against the Pagan Meccans for one reason alone, the survival of the faith of Islam. He had to fight because if there were no one alive to practice this way of life how would it have been able to survive to be given to the rest of the world. The pagan tribes of Mecca would have killed anyone and everyone who professed their belief in the faith of Islam. The early Muslims only fought to keep this faith alive so that the people of this age would be free to practice this same faith today. The wars fought by the Prophet (saw) were strictly defensive actions to maintain the life of Islam. The Muslims at that time were mercilessly being tortured and murdered for going against the beliefs of their pagan brothers. God gave Muhammad (saw) permission to fight only after he had endured years of persecution at the hands of the Meccans. Only after he had left his birthplace to escape persecution was he given permission to fight. Muhammad (saw) used fighting as the last resort to escape persecution for delivering his humble message. Even in fighting did the Prophet (saw) set the example of righteousness. He never attacked at night giving him the unfair advantage over his enemies. He ordered his followers not to kill the women during battle. He never burned crops or destroyed buildings. Even after his death the Khalifas set rules for conduct in battle. The European concept of "chivalry" that was acclaimed by the knights of Europe was learned from the Arabs. If an Arab soldier on horseback knocked his opponent of his horse the Arab would either help his enemy back onto his horse or fight his opponent on the ground in order to keep the fight fair.

The role of Khilafat still exists in the true followers of Islam. The divinely revealed institution of Khilafat still guides the Muslims on the path of righteousness and glory. Its beauty is still bright in today's clouded world and continues to guide millions of Muslims worldwide on the middle and right path.

Islam is all about morality and fairness even during times of war. The teachings of Islam should be preached and practiced by its exponents in order to create and maintain peace in the world. No practical example at least has been offered to show the world how non-violence can be applied when armed disputes arise between nation and nation or how non-violence can prevent or stop a war. To preach a method of stopping wars but never be able to afford practical illustration of that method indicates that the method is impracticable. It would therefore seem that human experience and wisdom point to only one method of preventing or stopping war and that method was taught and practiced by the Prophet of Islam (saw).

The Holy Prophet (saw) is reported to have said, "Whoever strangles himself strangles himself into fire, and whoever stabs himself with a spear stabs himself into fire." In Islam the only one that has the right to take a human life accept in extreme situations of self-defense is God alone. This means that man does not even posses the right to take his own life in any situation. Anyone who does is guilty of committing the most horrible of sins which is taking partners with God is definitely worthy of God's wrath. God often uses fire to describe punishment because one of the worst pains a man can ever experience is the feeling of being burned. Therefore God compares this terrible pain to the pain man would feel for disobeying His commandments. Suicide bombing is an act of desperation, insanity, and loss of hope. These poor souls are completely misguided, confused, and deceived by their leaders to believe they will be rewarded with heaven yet they will only be led to fire. These people are just as desperate as the Kamikaze fighter pilots of Japan during World War II. Suicide is a last act of desperation of solving your problems. Suicide is totally giving up on God and His assistance. People who resort to suicide bombing are so lost and have given up hope in God that they feel they must take their own life to make things better. What poor misguided souls!

Muhammad (saw) gave an excellent example of morality during peacetime as well as during times of war. The beauty of the Prophet Muhammad (saw) is that he is the perfect model for all mankind. Throughout the course of his short life he experienced everything a man could possibly experience. From being a poor man to building an empire. From living in times of peace to times of war. This is what made him so great. He experienced so much and gave mankind the perfect model for every situation. During the times of war the Prophet's (saw) leadership ability made him a superb general while his closeness to his men made them feel as though he was one of them. His courage in battle made him a strong warrior yet his compassion towards his prisoners made him honored and respected. All that he was, he gave praise and credit to God for all of it. His righteousness on the battlefield and during times of physical conflict made him an example of morality to his followers and his opponents. The faith he followed was so greatly shown through his actions that Islam swept across the Middle East with the speed that no sword could bring. Only through the kindness and morality of his good nature and the beauty of the faith he brought was Islam accepted by the masses not through violence, terror, or intimidation.

Western authors dare to say that Islam is still in the Middle Ages. To say Middle Ages for Islam is to try to compare Islam to Europe during the Middle Ages. The Middle Ages in Europe were a time of ignorance, violence, and desperation. Disease was rampant with nearly no cures to combat the various plagues. The wealthy lived lavishly while the poor starved. Only the monks could read while the serfs could barely write their own names. This was Europe at that time. To compare Islam to the Europeans at that time is pure lies. The Muslims at that time were of Arab descent since that is were the faith of Islam was perfected. With the advent of Islam the Arab culture was blessed in ways beyond the wildest dreams of Europe. The Arabs excelled in the field of medicine, astronomy, mathematics, and engineering. Education was of highest priority and schools of learning were built across the Arab lands. The Arab Muslims were making lunar calendars while the Europeans still believed the earth was flat.

Before Islam the Arabs were known for their warlike ways. The coming of Islam turned them into moral soldiers whose conduct in battle gave birth to the code of chivalry soon to be "adopted" by Europe. The Muslims moral code led them to be a very clean and hygienic conscious people. When the Muslims were being expelled from a country in Europe the European soldiers could tell who was Muslin or not by smelling the person and noticing if his neck was dirty from not bathing. The King ordered that all people should stop taking baths and using the soaps and perfumes that were introduced into the European society by the Arab Muslims. Those people who attempt to dirty the name of Islam by calling it medieval fail to compare it to the medieval days of Europe only making fools of themselves. Never at any time was or will Islam reach such a low point since this way of life is a divinely protected faith. God will never allow His teachings to disappear from the earth but will protect them by sending Prophets to continue to preach the Truth of Islam.

In the media the term "fundamentalist" has been used incorrectly. A fundamentalist is someone who follows the basics of a faith or concept. A fundamentalist Muslim follows all the teachings of Islam. An Islamic fundamentalist understands the teachings of Islam and does everything in his will to see that all the guidelines and rules of are carried out. There is nothing violent about being a fundamentalist of Islam. God intends that we all follow the fundamentals of this blessed message. Those who stray away from these simple fundamentals are not following the guidebook given to man and for this they will never prosper or see the rewards they seek so desperately to find. No political, financial, or military means can help those who stray from the fundamental guidelines that God has given. Only by following these fundamentals can one achieve success. The Promised Messiah Hadhrat Mirza Ghulam Ahmad of Qadian stated:

"The Qur'an is a living Book. It is not difficult for a reasonable and just person to understand that the purpose of a Book of God is to lead people to God, to make them believe in Him as a certainty, and to stop them from committing sin by impressing the majesty and awe of God upon their hearts. Of what use is a book, which cannot cleanse a heart, nor can bestow such pure and perfect understanding as should make one hate sin. The attraction of sin is a dangerous leprosy, which cannot be healed till the manifestation of the living and understanding God, and the signs of His awe and greatness and power, descend like rain and till a person perceives God with His terrible powers as a goat perceives a tiger, which is only two steps away from it. Man needs to be freed from the fatal passion of sin. The greatness of God should so occupy his heart that it should rid him of the overpowering desire of passion, which falls upon him like lightning and instantly consumes his store of righteousness. Those impure passions which attack repeatedly like epilepsy and destroy all sense of piety cannot be wiped out by a self conceived impression of God, nor can it be suppressed by ones own thinking, or be blocked by an atonement whose suffering has not been experienced by one. This is not a matter of indifference but in the estimation of a wise person it is worthy of consideration above all else as to how he might safeguard himself against the ruin which confronts him on accounts of his daring and his lack of relationship with God, the root of which is sin and disobedience.

It is obvious that a person cannot give up a certain pleasure for the sake of conjecture. It is only a certainty that can rescue one from another certainty. For instance, if we are certain that there are a number of deer in a forest whom we can easily catch, we are incited by that certainty to enter the forest for that purpose, but if we are also certain that there are a half a hundred lions in the forest and thousands of pythons, we would be dissuaded from making any attempt. Thus sin cannot be avoided without this degree of certainty. It is only iron that can break iron. There should be that certainty of the greatness and awe of God which should tear up the curtains of heedlessness, and make the body tremble, and should make death appear near. The heart should be so overcome by fear that all relationship with the sinful ego should be cut asunder and one should be drawn by hidden hands towards God and the heart should be filled with certainty that God Who is truly present does not leave a daring offender without punishment. What shall a seeker after true purity do with a book which does not fill this need?

God in whose meeting is man's salvation and eternal happiness cannot be found without following the Holy Qur'an. Would that people could see that which the Prophet of Allah has seen and they could hear that which he has heard and give up following stories and run towards reality. The means of obtaining perfect knowledge through which one can see God, and the cleansing water which removes all doubts, and the mirror through which one can behold that High Being, is the converse with God which has just been mentioned. He whose soul seeks the truth should arise and search for it. If souls were inspired by true search and hearts felt true thirst, people would look for this way and would search for it. Islam alone gives the good news of this way for other people have since long sealed up the possibility of revelation. Be sure that this seal is not set up by God, but as man has deprived himself of this favor, he seeks excuses for its absence. As it is not possible that we should be able to see without eyes or should be able to hear without ears or should be able to speak without a tongue, in the same way, it is not possible that we should be able to behold the countenance of the Beloved without the Holy Qur'an.

The Qur'an has the additional unique distinction among all other scriptures of being an entirely verbal revelation. That, in itself, is a guarantee that it would not be perverted or twisted. All non-Muslim scholars who have researched into the integrity of the text of the Holy Qur'an agree that it is an exact and accurate version of the verbal revelation that Muhammad, the Prophet of Islam, claimed that God had vouchsafed to him. This Divine guarantee of safeguarding the Qur'an is not confined to preserving the integrity of the text alone. It extends to all factors that bear upon the preservation of the Qur'an as the perfect source of Divine guidance for the whole of mankind, for all times. For instance, it is guaranteed that the language in which it was revealed, namely Arabic, would always continue to be a living language in current use, so that no difficulty might be met with in determining and comprehending the meaning of the Qur'an. Arabic is today spoken and written over a much greater area of the earth and by many hundred times the number of people than was the case when the Qur'an was revealed. Besides, the Holy Prophet predicted that at the beginning of every century, God Almighty would raise someone, from among his followers, who would set forth from the Qur'an the guidance that may be needed by mankind from time to time. In the case of no other scripture has the integrity of its text, its language and its guidance been maintained.

The Holy Qur'an is a rare pearl. Its outside is light and its inside is light and its above is light and its below is light and there is light in every word of it. It is a spiritual garden whose clustered fruits are within easy reach and through which streams flow. Every fruit of good fortune is found in it and every torch is lit from it. Its light has penetrated to hearts where it could have penetrated by no other means. If there had been no Qur'an there would have found no delight in life. Incline towards it with a great inclination and drink it into the heart. He who drinks from it comes to life and brings others to life."

Two objects cannot occupy the same space at the same time. It is not about bringing Islam into the modern world but what they really want to say is to bring Islam under Western culture, in turn, meaning idolatry. That will never happen. What will happen is that the Western world will be removed of Christianity and the other elements that have burdened the Western people and the beauty of Islam will replace it through logic and truth. This is the destiny of the people of the West. Not replacing it by force and violent means but through willful conversion of people who see and understand the light of this humble yet glorious way of life that is meant for all nations and tribes. Soon the people of the West will realize that this is the freedom they search for and it will elevate them to the heights that capitalism could never dream of and Christianity has no chance of doing. This way of life will give those in the West the reality it only dreams of. The acceptance of Christianity by the Romans was thought to be a very modern thing abandoning their many ancestral Gods and only worshiping three yet Christianity allowed them to keep their idols just giving them a facelift and a new name. Now the West is ready to take the next step to make a change of faith again. Islam is the next step that can ensure their future. Give up the idols and accept the One True God. This is the only way you will find the freedom and peace for which you yearn. Only by giving up these false gods that you have created will you be able to truly modernize yourselves, your community, and your people.

Modern is civilized and that is the opposite of barbaric. Barbarism is living like an animal and the only thing that guides us to not live like animals is morality. Morality is governed by spirituality and spirituality is governed by faith. Faith meaning the way of life. Since the worship of a man was the way of life that was practiced by different cultures around the globe centuries ago than how can one say that Christianity is a modern religion? Only by giving up those ancient ways of idolatry will true modernization begin in the Western world.

The Bible was meant for one group of people not White people. During the time of the Bible the teachings of Christ were not meant for the Romans. Christ himself talked about the White Romans referring to them as "dogs" and "swine" because of their animalistic ways at that time. Do you think he is going to want to be around the "dogs" and the "swine" a second time while they still practice the same lower qualities? Do you think it strange that Western people have said that a dog is man's best friend or that pork is Americas other white meat? Is this the same Christ who you are waiting to come back a second time? Do you think he is going to want to save the descendants of the Romans who hung him to die on the cross? The only universal prophet in the history of mankind is Muhammad (saw). The only universal faith ever sent by God is Islam. This message was given to lead Whites into the only way of life that is nearest to the commandments of God. The Qur'an is the only book that has the solutions to the problems of today with realistic applications. The few commandments of the Bible could in no way handle the excessive amount of hardships that the Western man has brought upon himself today. The moral way of life guided by the Qur'an is the only cure for the problems of today as well as tomorrow.

The New Testament spoke so much of love because it was given at a time when the group it was given to was in need of the message of compassion. This message of love was for the love of the fellow man. The people had strayed so far from the teachings of God that they needed a reminder that God was still with them and still loved them. Even though they had strayed so far from their teachings there was still a way to get back on the right track to pleasing their Creator. The time that the Bible was given was not a time for fighting or bloodshed but a time that justice would be proven through compassion and righteousness since the tribe it was revealed to was free to practice their religion in peace and in public without fear of persecution. This love was only for one group. Jesus was not Roman and cared not for the Romans as I have stated before. This love was only for one group and the White Romans were not that group then nor are they today.

Why give man the Qur'an or for that fact any revelation from God? The simple answer that I have chosen is one word. Guidance. Just as God has given man the correct tools to breathe God does not wish that man should have to struggle and search in the moral realm to find his way in life. God wishes to make things very easy on weak men like us. He has given us a map to follow to reach the moral and spiritual destination we search for everyday. Throughout the history of revealed faiths God has sent books to various prophets to utilize in the leading of the various tribes. The Qur'an is the ultimate book since it is the last and most complete book to be sent to mankind. It offers guidance on every aspect of human life that mankind will ever face. It not only shows how to avoid the harm of sin, but also gives historic instances of groups and tribes who disobeyed God and His commandments and tells of their horrific fates. God relates these stories so that men of today may not follow the same mistakes of the past ultimately leading to the same destruction. Man is a simple creature with a limited supply of knowledge. Since God knows how much knowledge man will ever get the Qur'an has been filled within its covers with enough information to combat all the problems and treacheries mankind will ever encounter. It is the perfect and complete guidance for all people to live by. Any subject you could have an interest in is contained within its 114 chapters so look for yourself and you will find that I tell only the truth.

Muhammad (saw) was known across the lands of the East for his greatness of forbearance in every aspect of his life. His forbearance towards his wives was shown towards each of them, treating them all with fairness and honesty. His forbearance towards his followers was show in his eagerness to help guide them all on the right path. His forbearance towards his persecutors was shown in his fairness even in battle. When he returned to Mecca, his birthplace, with ten thousand followers he meted out no vengeance towards those who persecuted him only a few years earlier.

Many Western writers say that the Old Testament was more violent than the New Testament. It is was not that the Old Testament was violent but it was written at a time when the people it was given to needed to rise up and fight for their freedom from physical enslavement. God knows that survival of the follower must be ensured for the purpose of the life of the faith. Only after years of enduring countless hardships did God give the enslaved people permission to stand and oppose their oppressors. The only acts of punishment were acts committed by God and to say that God made a violent action would be to say God is wrongfully cruel and that would be a complete lie since any physical punishment handed out by God is punishment well deserved. God has given man mercy after mercy and chance after chance to do the right thing yet man still chooses to do wrong. To judge God on His actions is terribly wrong of us weak mortals.

Western authors and leaders say that Islam oppresses the Middle East while it is only ignorant and greedy men who oppress the Middle East just as they oppress the North, South, and West. Foolish men use the lie that Islam oppresses only to make themselves look good and innocent. Islam is neither greed nor ignorance. They do this to hide the fact that it is they who truly oppress and hate the people of the Islamic world. The dictatorships that have risen in the Middle East have all been funded by Western nations. The misguided Muslim leaders have only taught an infected version of their faith only for their personal gain. Combine a power hungry madman with an outside government trying to control the Middle East you've got an anti-Islamic plot in the making. All the while you've got the knowledge-less people caught in the middle suffering the most as a result of these greedy forces on top of them. Only by returning to the true fundamentals of Islam and freeing themselves from the influence of the West will the Arab world be able to rid themselves of this yoke of oppression. Only by returning to prayer and the True Islam will they find freedom for their people.

The phrase "violent Islam" and "moderate Islam" are terms used by organizations that hate True Islam. The term "violent" is used to describe different groups of Muslims only to incite non-Muslims to hate the faith of Islam and those who follow it because of their violent actions. By using these violent murderers to be the examples of Islam it turns all non-Muslims against them while the real enemy is still the lack of true information. These organizations know that the weak poor nations of the Middle East are no physical threat to the massive military power of the West. During the time of Muhammad (saw), the beauty of Islam swept across the deserts of Arabia bringing morality and truth like wildfire and they know that even today the fire of Islam cannot be extinguished. This time around Islam will ignite the forests of the Western world and soon the European nations will be blessed with the beauty of the True Islam and the world will forever be changed. They know this, so they must try to use every tactic to combat the truth from freeing the people they have enslaved for so many centuries. They know that if they can make the Arab Muslims turn away from morality it will only help their cause of keeping the people of the West against Islam. But why would they want to keep people away from a faith that only claims peace? We'll answer that question later. "Moderate" sounds to me like half. Can half ever be as good as full? Even when saying "moderate," they are trying to insult Islam by saying it is not the complete way of life and that it still needs another half to complete its usefulness. Again they are way off the path of truth. Islam needs no other adjective to describe it.

Islam needs no other ideology to assist its cause or worth. Islam is the complete way of life that requires no assistance from any other form of faith to complete the circle of beauty, the credibility, and the usefulness it offers. As long as these organizations can keep the Western mind away from the freedom and blessings Islam contains within its body they will continue to keep the Western man under their thumb. The Western man has struggled for his existence through some of the harshest physical and moral times don't you think he deserves to rest and to be able to find a way of life that will be able to give him peace of mind as well as peace of body? Only Islam can fulfill that requirement. The Western people have always defined their struggles and conflicts through war so why not make their struggle with Islam seem to exist as a war also. Even then this still can never be considered a full war because a war can be won or loss while a war against God can never be won. A lie cannot last forever as long as mankind is always searching for the truth. As long as mankind grows tired of the lies and corruptions of the power structure of today they will always take one step closer towards Islam and the virtues it instills in man. One day that journey will be complete but will you be there to accept the reward? Today could be that day. I could spend hours on the different laws and guidelines that Islam gave to the Arabs almost 1,500 years ago that the Whites have just recently given priority in this society but that will be done another time.

MUHAMMAD

The correct term for one who practices Islam is Muslim not Muhammadan because it is not the laws and commandments of Muhammad (saw) that are to bowed down to but those of the One True God, the only object of worship. Muslims submit to the will of the One True God and no other. The Holy Prophet (saw) had the status of a Prophet and not that of a ruler upon this earth. He was the seal of the Prophets, i.e. the best and most perfect of the prophets, the last of the law-bearing prophets. Instead of being a monarch or an emperor of man Almighty God describes his status in the Holy Qur'an:

"And Muhammad is not the father to any men among you but he is only a messenger of God and the seal of the Prophets. And Allah is ever Knower of all things." (33:40)

Although his status was that of a Prophet of God and Seal of the Prophets there is no reason to doubt that from another aspect he could be aptly regarded as a king. His position in fact was so unique and multi dimensional that even the question and the debate whether he was a Prophet or king appears unnecessary. The Qur'an says:

"Verily, you have in the Prophet of Allah an excellent model." (33:22).

Muhammad (saw) was a perfect example for all walks of life. It was necessary that he should be given kingship also to enable him to demonstrate the supremacy of character and the perfection of behavior that should be associated with kingship. While exercising the responsibilities of a king he certainly remained innocent of the ill effects of character that sometimes accumulate in a person who is granted kingship. The opponents of Islam by presenting him in the line of worldly kings have done great injustices to his noble character. Kings are generally very fond of outward exhibition of pomp and show; in fact this is one of the primary means of expressing their all exalted status. The Holy Prophet (saw) however was absolutely free from all such trappings. The Holy Prophet (saw) was humbleness personified. Once he was offered to wear silk clothes and he replied, "Only he wears this who does not want any share from the life hereafter." (Bukhari). The Prophet (saw) slept on a coarse mattress so when asked why he replied, "I have no connection to this world; my relation with this world is only of a transitory kind like that of a rider who stops by a shady tree while traveling. He rests for a short while in the shade then takes off." (Jami Tirmidhi). A companion of the Prophet (saw) compared the luxury of the kings of Persia and Rome to the humble abode of the Prophet yet he replied, "Would you not like that they take this world and I get the hereafter?" (Sahih Muslim).

In ordinary dealings and conversation, worldly kings have a peculiar style of ceremony and grandeur. The Holy Prophet (saw) while talking with thousands never let them feel as though they were conversing with a superior person and was so down to earth that he appeared as a normal person. Once he came out of his house and the companions who were waiting outside stood up as a mark of respect upon which he said, "Do not stand up like the people of Ajam, i.e. as is customary of non-Arabs, on seeing me." (Abu Daud). Have worldly kings ever bowed so low in humility? In the early days of his Prophethood he went to propagate the faith of Islam to a group of people but they stoned him so bad his feet began to bleed. Although he had been divinely told of their destruction the Prophet begged God for their forgiveness. After he returned to Mecca at the head of ten thousand followers he forgave his tormentors for their ill treatment of the Muslims only punishing a few who murdered Muslims. His forgiveness and leniency shown to his deadliest opponents was unique and not found anywhere else in recorded history.

Worldly kings are greedy to add to their piles of riches while Muhammad (saw) was exactly the opposite. Money and riches came to him in abundance yet he never let a night pass without distributing them to his followers. He is quoted as saying, "If the mountain of Uhad turns into gold for me, I will not let three nights pass with even a dinar for me." (Buhkari). Earthly kings strive their utmost that after their death their family should continue in luxury. The Holy Prophet (saw) advised his relatives to follow righteously and live simple humble lifestyles. Worldly kings are usually very fond of flattery and praise yet the Prophet of Islam was exactly the opposite. Once a companion called him master and the Prophet quickly forbade the use of such titles. He was never called emperor or king by his followers, built himself a throne or castle, or kept bodyguards like the kings of Europe. Such was not Muhammad (saw) the like of whom the world never knew before nor would it ever witness again till the end of time. The language of history is such that no impartial person can ignore accept at his own doing. Nothing ever changed his lifestyle or his frugal habits even when he became the undisputed ruler of the whole of the Arabian Peninsula. Despite better conditions he spent little on his family less upon himself and much more on charity.

The two major sources of teaching in Islam are the Qur'an, the word of God, and Sunnah, the practices of the Holy Prophet Muhammad. The Qur'an is the revealed word of God that contains all the teachings that man requires to be able to exist in this world. The Sunnah are the practices of the Holy Prophet based on the teachings of the Qur'an so they must exactly follow the Qur'an. The Qur'an is still the ultimate word of Islam since it is the exact word of God. Any information needed about Islam is found in the Qur'an making it the first and last word for Islam. If the information you seek is not found in the Qur'an then it is neither a part of Islam nor condoned by Islam.

It is so easy to see the hatred of Islam shown in the works of countless non-Muslim authors. Their hatred and jealousy of the greatness of Islam and its victories on as well as off the battlefield has no bounds. I hope that one day they will be released of their anger. Throughout European history the greatest heroes have been those who fought till the death on the field of battle for their cause. Most of the saints in the Christian faith were soldiers who fought mercilessly in the defense of Christianity. Yet when it comes to the heroes of Islamic history, they make an attempt to defame and destroy their feats of dedication and strength; an attempt that will never succeed.

The story of the Two Eagles is no different and only the truth of this episode of Islamic history will forever shield it from so many vicious liars. When the Holy Prophet (saw) was forced to leave Mecca he decided to settle in Medina. Islam had already spread to this city and there was a fairly large Muslim community when he arrived there. More and more people joined the fold of Islam. Soon Medina became the first Muslim city.

When the pagan Meccans learned that the Prophet (saw) had been warmly received by the people of Medina and that Islam was making progress among the tribes they resolved to attack Medina. They raised an army of one thousand armed fighters, most of who were well experienced in warfare, and started marching towards Medina, one year after the Holy Prophet (saw) reached there. When the news reached the Holy Prophet (saw) he took counsel with his people and gathered 313 men to fight the enemy. Most of these men had no experience in fighting. Some of them were mere boys in their teens. The Muslims were ill equipped. There were only two horses and a few camels among the lot. As this was the first battle between the Muslims and the non-believers every Muslim fighter, young and old, was eager to show his bravery in battle. All of them were determined to die in defense of their faith. Such was the motley crew, led by the Holy Prophet (saw) which came out to meet the enemy. The two forces met at a place called Badr.

One of the few experienced fighters on the Muslim force was Abdul Rahman bin Auf. He was prepared because the day he was longing for had come. He could show his skill and valor on the battlefield. As the Holy Prophet (saw) arranged the Muslims for the battle Abdul Rahman looked towards his side and was greatly disappointed to see two young boys on either side of him. He felt exposed on both sides and would have to take good care of himself. As he was contemplating the situation, one of the boys nudged him and said, "Uncle where is Abu Jahl, who used to persecute the Holy Prophet and harass the Muslims?"

Abdul Rahman had not yet shown him Abu Jahl, when the other boy on the other side whispered the same question in his ear. Abdul Rahman raised his finger in order to point out Abu Jahl, who was on horseback, well armed and right in the heart of the Meccan army.

No sooner did Abdul Rahman point out Abu Jahl than the two boys dashed forward into the ranks of the enemy with the speed of an eagle. The attack was so sudden that everybody was shaken. The soldiers and guards round Abu Jahl were taken by surprise. They attacked the boys in order to prevent them from going further towards their leader. One of the boys received blows on his shoulder. His arm was cut and hung loose by his side, yet he continued to fight with one hand. The other boy was also injured, but they did not retreat. They went on and on until they reached Abu Jahl. They pounced upon him with such force that the experienced commander fell to the ground, and was fatally wounded. The two young brave Muslim boys did what surprised even the best among the Muslim fighters.

This situation occurred during a time of war no different than the Revolutionary War or the Vietnam War when two opposing armies were thick in the midst of deadly combat. During times of war a death of a solider is never called a murder but is called a casualty so why should the situation with these two young soldiers be anything different? It is called something different only out of hatred and jealousy against Islam and the courage it instills in those fighting for their faith. Remember it is only because the Muslims were saying they believed in One God that the pagan Meccans were trying their hardest to annihilate them from the face of the earth. When we hear of other races of people being killed because of their religion we offer our hardiest sympathies but for the Prophet and his weak followers we have no pity? This was not just a random slaying that occurred during peacetime but a casualty during hand-to-hand combat. Many parents have lost sons during battle while fighting for the American cause and have received flags and medals in their fallen sons honor so why should those two boys be any different? How many young boys fresh out of high school joined the service to go kill the enemy during World War II anxious to show their bravery in defense of their country? Shouldn't one be just as courageous and ready to defend his religion as the followers of Muhammad (saw) were?

Many liars wish to proclaim loudly the so-called "bloody" exploits of Muhammad (saw) and Islam but fail to acknowledge that these battles were only fought in the defense of religious freedom. Muhammad (saw) never fought over land like the Roman Caesar, or over money like George Washington, or over greed and like Napoleon. Muhammad (saw) only fought in defense of this divinely revealed faith. Man makes so many reasons to wage merciless wars using weapons of such destructive power that the very earth seems ready to crack under their tremendous force while the insane reasons they use to explain why they are causing such mass destruction of human life are accepted and honored. When it comes to a man defending his faith he is deemed insane but if it is over money the excuse is accepted. Is your property more important than your faith or do you love your money more than your God?

My Western family when will you understand that it is not Islam that is the enemy but those whose hatred of the beauty of Islam that is the true enemy. Ignorance is the enemy. Lack of knowledge and immorality are enemies who stand to prosper and exist from these immoral ways. It is these enemies who force vices upon you and your children who are the true foe no matter which race they belong to. Only by giving up the old ways of worshiping men and idols will the people of the West be able to truly understand that it is not the color of a man, or the way he dresses, that makes him good or bad but it is the true contents of his heart and mind which determines whether he is friend or foe. Only after this true awakening will the curtains be pulled back to reveal the true enemy.

Non-Muslim scholars often give biased accounts of Islam and its teachings: But what else can be expected? Would a vegetarian give a t-bone steak thumbs up or would he condemn the eating of a fine piece of meat? All men are allowed to make their own decisions and statements but only through the investigation of one's own research will man be able to find the true answers to his questions. Authors and writers are going to say what they want their readers to believe not necessarily the truth. Just as companies do heavy research on their customer base before selling a product so have authors in the process of publishing books. As long as the public opinion towards something goes one way the authors will continue to write the same way so they can make the money they want to make. Would it make sense for a non-Muslim author to write positive things about Islam? Would it make sense for a vegetarian magazine to promote the buying and selling of lamb chops?

If the readers do not like the content of the publication they will not buy the book and the author will not make any money. The non-Muslim authors who continue to print false misleading lies about Islam only do it to keep Western readers away from the beauty of Islam and to keep filling their pockets with your money. If you are going to buy a book please make sure you are buying the correct information. I can't say it enough, do the research and you will find the correct information.

MARRIAGE

The Prophet (saw) was the perfect example for all men to follow because he lived every scenario a man could be put in throughout the short course of his mortal life. One of the many stages man should go through in his life is the institution of marriage. The Prophet (saw) displayed an excellent example of how a husband should treat his wife. The taking of more than one wife is a custom practiced by many nations around the world. Having more than one wife is only allowed in countries were it is legal. Islam teaches that one should follow the law of the land. Marriages that are not recognized by the state are not recognized in True Islam. The allowance of more than one wife is acceptable during certain situations and thus through the life of Muhammad (saw) he married more than one wife in order to prove and show man that even when married to more than one bride one could still live a moral and God fearing life. However, he stated that no man should have more than four wives at once. He also stated that if a man does not think that he can treat them with all with equal kindness that he should not take more than one. The acceptance of more than one bride was accepted in many cultures of the world. This practice was condoned in many cultures due to the fact that wars often broke out and the lack of males due to deaths in times of war left many women husbandless and alone. Thus allowing men to marry more than one bride if they were mentally and financially competent for the woman's protection and keep.

Women could be provided for, protected, and able to keep their moral honor thus lowering the need for such vices as adultery and prostitution. Islam does not say that every man must marry more than one wife because God knows that every man does not have the proper physical or mental capabilities to ensure the successfulness of maintaining multiple marriages. God knows that these times may arise and through His unlimited guidance teaches man the proper way to carry out the responsibilities of marriage whether to one wife or four. Islam gives man the knowledge to stabilize and improve his moral status within himself, his family, his community, and the world. The marrying of more than one wife helps to protect the honor of women spiritually as well as their physical safety. The marrying of more than one wife is only meant as a safety device for the moral upliftment of the society not to use women as sexual toys only to satisfy the husband's sexual inhibitions.

Islam holds very high respect for the honor and security of women and offers the solutions for maintaining a highly moral and safe society for men and woman alike. Islam does not cater to one sex over another but provides equal responsibility in the male and the female for the maintaining of a highly moral society. The Western nations of today have chosen to think this practice as barbaric and anti-feminist yet the numbers speak for themselves on the outrageous amount of prostitution, adultery, pornography and other sexually related crimes found here in the Western world. The anti-Islamic organizations are blind to the moral rewards of marrying more than one wife because they are so blindly focused on the physical greed of their own minds. They cannot see the moral rewards that Islam offers a society whose ratio of women to men is not balanced. Islam is a faith that is designed to ensure that all parts of the society are able to control their inner demons thus making the community safe, moral, and productive.

The splendors of this world could be obtained and were not forbidden to any Muslim but such transitory vanities were not to be admitted into the household of God's Prophet (saw). The Holy Prophet Mohammad (saw) chose to live very humbly and therefore his wives also lived in this condition. At one point in time there was talk amongst them desired more of the goods of this world's life that they saw there husband giving away as soon as they came in the door. It appears that two of the Prophets' wives demanded these goods and later the others joined in and when the Prophet (saw) upon receiving Divine revelation gave an option to his wives either to remain in his household without the worldly comforts or to part company with him and have the desired worldly comforts, the Prophet (saw) told his first wife not to make a decision without consulting her parents. As he possessed the means, his wives would be allowed to depart with rich and ample gifts, if such was their desire. After the incident, they all united in their decision to remain in the house of the Prophet (saw) without the worldly provisions. This shows that all the qualifications which are mentioned here were met by the Prophets' (saw) wives. He had been given the choice to divorce any of his wives whom he did not desire but when the wives decided not to leave him he did not divorce any of them.

This verse clearly shows the complete obedience of the Prophet (saw) to the command of God and his compassion towards his wives feelings when he offered them the chance to divorce him rather then have them unhappy. This verse clearly shows his caring and respect for his wives while showing his undying obedience to his Creator. His perfect example shows man that even though God is the Lord and Master second to that is the treatment of our fellow man as long as it does not violate the laws of God. The Christian Western values of marriage differ quite often from the values of marriage in Islam. The Holy Qur'an says,

"He it is who has created you from a single soul and made there from its mate, that he might find comfort in her. So when he covers her she bears a light burden then moves about with it. Then when it grows heavy, they both call upon Allah, their Lord: if Thou givest us a good one, we shall certainly be of the grateful." (7:189).

This verse signifies that marriage is meant for the attainment of peace of mind, mutual love, affection, and procreation. God also says that marriage is a means of attaining piety and of guarding ones chastity. The Qur'an says,

"...They are a sort of garment for you and you are a sort of garment for them." (2:188).

The mutual relations of husband and wife are here described in words which could not be surpassed in beauty. In these preceding words, we are told that while satisfying a natural desire, the relation of husband and wife has higher ends in view. They serve as a garment for each other, i.e. they serve as a means of protection, comfort, and even embellishment for each other while the weakness of one is made up by the strength of the other. A better way of teaching communication, trust, and teamwork in a marriage has never been found in the history of the world nor will one be created in the future. Since the Qur'an uses the word "garment" in respect of both husband and wife it proves beyond a shadow of a doubt that they hold an equal status so while their rights and duties are identical in respect of each other they are both bound to fulfill their obligations to each other. These duties are:

1. To cover up ones weaknesses from others.

2. To act as an adornment and embellishment for each other.

3. To support the other.

According to the Islamic point of view marriage is not an ordinary combination of two opposite sexes nor is it only to quench ones sexual desires. Marriage is rather a holy union of two inevitable life companions on whose virtue or vices rest the prosperity or the disaster of human society. Marriage in Islam means laying the foundation of a fabric from which emerges a benevolent and beneficial society and therefore it enjoins upon every Muslim to marry. The Prophet Muhammad (saw) said, "O company of the youth! He who can afford to marry should marry, for it keeps the eyes cast down and keeps the man chaste; and he who cannot afford to marry should take to fasting for it will have a sobering affect upon him." According to this tradition it is quite clear that the purpose of marriage in Islam, as far as society is concerned, is to keep society chaste, healthy, and pure from grossness and immorality. A man who can afford to marry and yet refrains to marry must definitely be led to immorality and will be a nuisance to society which we observe clearly as due to the problems of the so called modern civilizations of the world.

The second thing that Islam says in regard to marriage is that it has lasting effects. The responsibility of supporting the family has been laid upon the male. The responsibility of the well being of the children and their training has been laid upon the female. If the woman is chaste, pious, and religious she would bring up the children in a well-trained manner and thus society emerging from those children would be highly moral and respectable. The main object of Islam is that purity and piety should be imbedded in the practice of the Muslim to the extent that their character would be impeccable and faultless. Islam does not allow a guardian to force the to be bride or groom to accept his choice. The Holy Prophet (saw) said, "The widow shall not be married until she is consulted and the virgin shall not be married until her consent is obtained."

The duties of a wife are as follows:

1. To look after the comfort of her husband, give him due respect and always have regard for his feelings.

2. To safeguard the honor of her husband.

3. To guard the property of her husband.

4. To rear and bring up their children properly.

5. Treat the relatives of her husband as if they were her own.

6. To beautify herself for her husband.

7. To bear in mind the tastes of her husband in the matter of food and dress.

8. To be ever mindful of her husband's health.

9. To give her most sincere advice when her husband consults her in any of his problems.

10. To remain loyal to her husband under all conditions and be a source of strength to him in adverse conditions.

11. Not make unreasonable and unfair demands on the purse of the husband.

12. To be careful that the dignity and reputation of her husband are not harmed by her actions.

13. That her behavior should be conducive to peace in the house.

In Islam the responsibilities of the husband are also very clearly defined. The duties of a husband are as follows:

1. To respect and be very mindful of the susceptibilities of his wife.

2. To be a source of comfort to his wife and behave in a manner that convinces her that she alone is the center of his love and affection.

3. To provide for all her reasonable needs and keeping within his means and should be disposed to spending in that respect with an open hand.

4. To participate in the management of the house by giving hand in the household chores.

5. To look after her health and always be anxious about it.

6. To refrain from keeping a close watch over every movement of his wife as if he had no confidence in her and thus making her life miserable.

7. To be disposed to overlooking the minor shortcomings of his wife and be generous in forgiving and forgetting.

8. He should see that trifles do not lead to a situation in which tempers are lost and threats of divorce are pronounced.

9. He should shun every act which is likely to displease his wife.

10. To display a sense of utmost sympathy towards his wife when she is in distress or misfortune.

11. Not object to his wife meeting her relatives provided no mischief is feared from their side. He should be respectful to them.

12. To consult his wife in all family matters of importance and handle the situation as decided by mutual consent.

13. If more than one wife, the husband must treat them equally in every respect, in dress, in food, in living accommodations, and in the duration of his stay with each of them.

Islam gives strict distinctions to the roles of men and women. Men and women possess different physical and anatomical structures. The distinctive duties of the woman and man are clarified in the Islamic code of life. These different duties have been assigned in order to maintain a moral society, to withstand the formation of sin within the community, and for the physical and moral upliftment of those within it. The duties vary according to the sex because each sex has built in tools that make them fit and ready to perform the task assigned to him or her. Would you use a hammer to cut wood or a saw to bang nails into the wall? God knows about these tools because He is the one who downloaded the appropriate programs into the appropriate sex. Would God want His tools to be used in a way He did not design it for? Would the tool be able to be used to its maximum efficiency? This distinction between the functions of man and woman is only part of God's plan to give us the easiest and most complete way for mankind to live a moral and productive life. As long as these boundaries continue getting crossed and mixed it will be as the unraveling of a thread of yarn, confusion for all those within it.

HUMAN RIGHTS IN ISLAM

The West claims to hold the monopoly on human rights. The rights of Western society are whatever rights are in fashion at that time. A right is given to a people only because those who are in power expect to receive something back from those rewarded the rights. Are the rights being given because they are due or merely out of greed for power? Just because these rights are given does the one in power really care about the rights of others or just his personal wealth? In order for complete human rights to be given, everyone must abandon all thoughts of power and control of others and greed for wealth. Has the Western society done this? The problem with the Western world is that they have become obsessed with themselves and their accomplishments so they feel they have outrun God and His Judgment. The European race has never been known for the human rights it has given to other races. The atrocities and injustices of the Europeans are too many to name but just in case you slept through history class: the genocide of nearly an entire race of Americans, the slaughter of millions of Jews in Germany, the enslavement and murder of Africans, etc.

Name a time in history when the European race has done something for another people clearly out of love for their fellow humans? I am not speaking of individuals. There are many who have and continue to take part in selfless acts. Every race of people is guilty of this fault but why is it that the White race feels they have overcome this human fault when they not only perpetrate this crime but also are the main instigators of this ideology today?

The Qur'an is a Book of warning to all people. The Qur'an warns not just people of the Arab race but also people of all races concerning the reactions of their actions. God knows the response to all and any acts committed by man now till forever. Man is very limited in its imagination of wrongdoings and only requires a limited guidebook to keep him on the right path. The Qur'an clearly shows God's mercy as He has given exact rules by which to live and conduct our lives. God has handed us the reward on a silver platter so all we must do is obey the laws He has put in place. We obey the laws of the government yet we disobey the laws of God! Who do you think is more important and demands a more complete obedience? Who do you think will hand out punishment of a more violent and terrible nature?

We know to slow down at a yellow light but when other signs are shown to us we ignore them. While the rest of the world despises the West we do nothing to investigate the cause of their hatred. The universe is guided by cause and effect. By turning the blind eye you only seal your fate more and more. Every time you try to take a step forward your leaders only drag you back five steps. When will you wake up to free yourselves from the bondages of these wannabe gods? Your false idols will only bring you more pain and destruction. While your leaders sit comfortably behind steel and concrete bunkers, you will be the ones to suffer for their arrogance and deceit leaving you to feel the flames of the lies your taxes funded.

The major difference between the concept of hell in Islam and hell in Christianity is that in Islam God tells man that hell is not forever while Christianity dooms man to hell for eternity. The God of the Qur'an is slow in handing out punishment. Man pays the price for each wrong act committed either in this life or the next. Once this price is paid God ultimately forgives man of his wrongs and admits him to Paradise. Does this sound like the merciless God of Islam that so many misguided writers have proclaimed Him to be? God knows that man in his weakness often needs to be punished yet even the wrath of God is handed out with fairness and equality. Hell is a place of reform that so that the soul may be shown the error of his ways resulting in a punishment demanded by the severity of his crimes. In Islam it is believed that heaven and hell start here in the physical world. These places of reward or punishment are the natural reactions that happen to a person when he commits an act of good or wrongdoing. The laws of nature are put in place so that for every action a person commits there is an equal reaction.

Hell is the result of a sinner's free will. The freedom of choice is the greatest gift God has bestowed on mankind yet with this great reward comes great responsibility. The responsibility is that we must each regulate our freedom of choice to do good deeds and to avoid lesser ones. However that is not the case here in the Western nations. This freedom has been disguised to make people think that this freedom allows them to commit acts stated as creative or curious. These acts are committed just because the physical power to do them exists. Although man has this power of choice he is blinded by the simple physical pleasures he receives for committing these immoral acts. If man wants the rewards of his actions he should also be willing to accept the punishment of his actions. Parents get so upset when their daughters get pregnant yet it was them who pushed dating upon their daughters or bought them the makeup and revealing clothes to wear only to excite the sexual stimuli of the males they are around. Fathers become enraged when boys look at their daughters as they walk through the mall but it is them who allow their daughters to come out of the house half-naked.

"Seest thou not those who change Allah's favor for disbelief and make their people to alight in the abode of perdition." (14:28).

People must learn that Jesus Christ will not be the one to receive the punishment caused by man's actions and that they alone are responsible for the actions they commit, condone, and allow. The false theory of Salvation will only allow them to get closer and closer to pain and misery today and tomorrow.

"And upon Allah it rests to show the right way and there are some deviating. And if He please, He would guide you all aright." (16:9).

In the Western society where freedom is such a cherished thing you would think that the White race would be the first to see the beauty of the Qur'an where freedom is so often mentioned. God also tells men that those ways that are not his way are the wrong paths and that men should avoid them all together. God is telling us this because He knows that by not following the path that He has laid out for man he will only suffer for the mistake of turning away from the right path. Islam is the only religion that claims to be the right path for all people. God goes on to explain that it was Him who gave man the free will to make his own decisions and choose his own paths whether they are the right path of God or the wrong path of devastation. God in His own greatness and power could have made us all believers but even He in His Majesty has given mankind the freedom to choose his own path. Thus man will not be able to say it was God who brought His punishment upon them. Only by their own doings have they been punished. God gives man the ultimate lesson in responsibility allowing no one to take the blame for the actions of another. Even though God is the All Powerful He is not a forceful God but a Giving Nurturing being who even in His Glory, He is Humble.

The Qur'an gives a blessing and a warning for all men when discussing the punishment of the next life. When a child commits a wrongdoing doesn't the parent explain how he is going to be disciplined? Whether it is a verbal or physical punishment a precise explanation is always given to the child on what disciplinary action is going to be taken. In the beginning of every school year pamphlets are given to students to remind them of the punishments of offenses they might commit. Teachers do that so the child understands what type of punishment he is going to receive if he ever commits that action again. The Qur'an is God's way of explaining the punishment mankind will receive for committing acts against the commandment of God. These verses also serve as a warning of the punishment mankind will bring upon itself here in this physical life by committing unlawful acts. If God did not tell mankind what his punishment would be man would not fear the wrath of God and would live a life of disregard and immorality because of the lack of fear of punishment from the Almighty. Hell has been described in physical terms in all religions because the physical world is all that we can comprehend. It is likened mostly with burning fires or the swallowing of boiling water. God does not tell man of hell's fire for His own benefit but for the benefit of mankind. This knowledge of hell is a blessing because it gives us the inspiration to do good to avoid the heat of hell's flames. Instead of questioning God's reason behind telling us of hell we should thank Him for telling us about it so that we may strive harder to avoid it.

For men to continue to insult God by saying that He is delighted at the failure of man is ludicrous. If God really wanted men to suffer He wouldn't have the carbon dioxide level in the air we breathe exactly the percentage it is. He would have made the molecules in the water poisonous instead of life giving. He would have made the UV rays from the sun more potent then they are. God has given man all that he needs to survive so to say that God takes delight in men going to hell is illogical and stupid. God doesn't need man to give Him delight because He needs nothing nor any one to fill His needs. Even though some of the Qur'an discusses the punishment for our misdeeds the spirit of the Qur'an is mercy stating that God is the most merciful of all beings. God constantly reminds man of His ever-encompassing mercy. The first verse of every chapter but one in the Qur'an states, *"In the name of Allah, the Gracious, the Merciful."*

Many misguided authors say the Qur'an is too graphic in detail in regards to the punishment of misdeeds. But is the Qur'an as graphic as the music we allow our children to listen to on their stereos. Does its contents come close in explicitness as the music videos they watch on TV or the video games you buy for them to play? Does this book compare to the violence that occurs in our nation's schools or athletic events? Does the Qur'an come close in sexual content as thousands of under 18 single mothers that are burdened with the responsibilities of raising children? Turn on the TV and I guarantee on half of the channels during anytime of the day you can find half naked people prancing around performing simulated sexual acts. I mean lets be honest does the Qur'an allow your 15 year old daughter to date some 17 year old sexually excited teenage boy? Do you know what that boy expects from your daughter and what kinds of acts he's asking your daughter to perform? But yet you condone and even promote their dating, proms, and other acts of male female inter-mixing only leading them closer to performing these immoral acts.

The Qur'an was revealed to the Prophet (saw) while living in Arabia. Prior to the coming of the messenger the Arabian nomads were known throughout the world as men without fear who were quick to fight and kill over anything. Once a war waged between two tribes for years over a bet on a camel race. The Arabians were so violent that it was reported that after they would kill an enemy they would cut out his liver and eat it, raw. If the Arabians were to receive discipline from God it could not be some little sissy punishment that they would just laugh at and take for granted. These were a people who killed for sport and only a punishment of Godly repercussion would be able to inflict a fear of Godly respect from such a merciless group of warriors. This guidance is also definitely needed today with violence as rampant as it is here in the West. This Holy Book is just as needed today as it was needed in pre-Islamic Arabia. Killing over nothing has erupted like a volcano on the streets of America. Violence in the domestic front results in deaths, dismemberments, and rape. Gang wars spill blood in the urban as well as the suburban neighborhoods of the West. Audio and visual violence and sexual explicitness is broadcast all day. Just as in the days prior to the coming of Muhammad (saw) the violent nature of man has run rampant. Just as in the days of pre-Islam today's youth have become unafraid of the punishment of God because they feel they have the power to give and take human life. They can purchase a gun down the street or listen to the same music sung by criminals.

We have allowed our youth to think that the power of God is nothing and the illusion of power of man is all encompassing and all-powerful. Only through the guidance of the Qur'an can we switch these roles of power back to where they really are and save our children from the gunfire of automatic weapons and other violence in our streets today and the torments of hell's fire in the next life. People who are hateful of God and his awesome truths have tried to paint this horrible portrait of God yet they try in every way to imitate His awesome strength for their own personal or gain. They only do this because they want to be God yet they know they never will. They know that in the end they will receive the exact same punishment they said God could not give. Since man has mortalized God they have taken away his strength and majesty and weakened Him to barely nothing. That is why man is not afraid to commit the horrendous acts he does. He has no fear of God punishing him. They think that because God does not strike them dead for committing those acts that they think God is weak and they are stronger. In the end who will always die and be brought before who for judgment?

Did God create man or did man create God? What right does man think he possesses that he can tell God not to judge the non-believers? Or is it that the non-believers know they have messed up so badly that this is their way of begging God for His forgiveness? Even when they know they are doing something wrong they don't stop it so what makes them think they deserve anything from God when they are constantly going against His wishes? The Western prison population is the largest in the world. So for a country that boast that other countries hate them because of their freedom, it seems that the freedom to commit horrendous crimes and yet be shown more affection then the victims is one of those freedoms. How does this lack of respect for the law and a prison system that rivals better living than those on the outside of its barbed fences effect a youngster who is tempted to enter into a life of crime? A criminal knows that his punishment will only be a slap on the wrist and the deterrent from committing that crime shrinks smaller and smaller. Instead of building a society of law abiding citizens it only creates a community of non-fearing criminals. We in the United States hear everyday "God bless America" but why should He bless America? What has it done to deserve blessings? In my opinion we should be saying "God forgive America." By recognizing the mistakes made on American soil and stopping them from happening again is the only way America will be blessed by God. God is very logical so He does not reward those who behave against His will. The West is definitely disobedient to the will of God. Would you as a parent reward your disobedient child so why wouldn't you expect God to do the same?

"*The only punishment of those who wage war against Allah and His Messenger and strive to make mischief in the land is that they should be murdered, or crucified, or their hands and their feet should be cut off on opposite sides, or they should be imprisoned. This shall be a disgrace for them in this world, and in the Hereafter they shall have a grievous chastisement.*" (5:33).

The words used here spoke originally to all those opponents of Islam who waged war on Muhammad (saw) and the early Muslims and made mischief in the land by murdering innocent Muslims and destroying their property. This commandment has also been accepted as meaning all murderers who cause disorder in a settled state of society whether a thousand years ago or today. In fact when war came to an end in Arabia and Islam was established over the whole peninsula the enemies of Islam being unable to oppose authority openly resorted to murder and brutality to disturb peace which was now established in the land. Hence, though it is such enemies that are spoken of here the words also include all cases of murder and terrorism.

The four different types of punishment clearly show that the punishment to be handed out depends on the circumstances surrounding the crime. The judge must take all the circumstances into consideration and inflict a fair yet effective punishment to ensure the safety of the society. Islam teaches fairness toward the criminal but also ensures the safety and prosperity of the citizens of the community. This commandment pertains to those vicious criminals who desire to cause death and mayhem. The method of dealing with this criminal element is needed because if the purpose of mankind is to praise God how can man worship his creator if he is in constant fear of being killed? The fear of a murderous death overtakes the society and they soon begin to worship their fears instead of focusing on the One True God. No society should live in mortal fear of being persecuted or murdered so God through His ultimate wisdom has given man all the guidance he needs to live in comfort even when difficult situations may arise so that they may be taken care of quickly and fairly.

Many Christian and Western writers have made claims that Islam preaches to accept Islam or die. Nowhere in the Qur'an or Hadith (sayings) of the Prophet (saw) does it say accept Islam or die. Not one verse says become Muslim or meet death. This is a made up belief in the minds of misguided people. This is merely lie invented by liars to keep men away from the beauty of Islam. Don't take my word for it read the Qur'an yourself and you will see the truth about this ignorant lie.

"O you who believe, oppose those of the disbelievers who are near to you and let them find firmness in you. And know that Allah is with those who keep their duty." (9:123).

"O Prophet, strive hard against the disbelievers and the hypocrites and be firm against them. And their abode is hell, and evil is the destination." (9:73).

The Prophet is commanded to strive and exert himself against the disbelievers and the hypocrites yet nowhere does it mention a sword or any other physical tool or weapon. The Prophet is commanded here to use ones' most utmost power in contending with an object of disapproval against the disbelievers as well as hypocrites. This only means that he must continue to preach with no rest to both the disbelievers and the hypocrites but nowhere in the Qur'an does it condone or praise the killing of men, women or children just because they are non-Muslim.

There are some verses that discuss fighting. There are very strict guidelines as to when war is permissible. It is only in retaliation and even then there are further stipulations. These were revealed during the times of persecution and torture from the pagan Meccans. The commandment to fight back was given to the Prophet (saw) so that he could stop the merciless persecution and murder of the innocent Muslims whose only deed was the worship of the One True God. The verses commanded the Muslims to remain steadfast because they were so outnumbered by the Meccans and they did not posses one third of the military might of the disbelievers that the Muslims only motivation to fight was for the blessings of Allah. They stood to gain nothing nor wanted anything in return.

All the authors and leaders who say that killing is what Islam teaches have no clue as to what Islam is truly about. Islam gives no Muslim the right to harm innocent men, women, or children. The chapter which these two verses come from is called Al-Bara which means, The Immunity. This chapter declares immunity from obligations the early Arab Muslims made with the disbelievers after the non-Muslim Meccans had violated the treaties they had in place. The Muslims suffered heavy losses due to the breaking of these treaties so God gave the Muslims this declaration of immunity so it was impossible for the Muslims to be bound by these treaties and the terms of the agreements while the enemies constantly attacked and killed them. The Muslims under this declaration were to stand firm under the treaties as long as the other party adhered to the terms. This chapter tells Muslims of the sacrifices they would have to make in the cause of the Truth but goes on to tell of the victory of Islam. The chapter ends with God telling the Muslim community that they must contribute men to carry the message of Truth to the whole world. That is the real object of Islam. This chapter was revealed during one of the harshest times of the Prophets life so these verses were given to the Prophet to ensure that the Muslims did not feel abandoned by God to leave them to be slaughtered by the enemy. Nowhere in the Qur'an does it allow random murder of non-Muslims. The Qur'an prohibits murder. The Qur'an gives only the government the right to hand out punishment to the murderer as long as the punishment is just and not beyond the precepts of morality. The Qur'an prohibits vigilantism. Nowhere in the Qur'an does it give the Muslim the right to commit murder for any reason.

Only the West has made the Taliban or Al Quieda the voice of Islam. How can the Taliban say they are the voice of Islam when so many of their actions go exactly against the Holy Qur'an and the teachings of the Holy Prophet? Only the enemies of Islam would use the Taliban to represent Islam because this is what they want you to think Islam is about. Do you think that McDonalds is going to say good things about Wendy's? People who endorse their way of life will never say good things about the competition because they fear they will loose their followers to the ways of the other side. It's all about keeping followers. It is all about control and power although they fail to tell you that the only true power and control belongs to the One True God. That is where the truth gets lost and the lies rise to the surface. Would you use a murderer to be the voice of Christianity then why allow a murderer as the voice of Islam?

"O you who believe, intoxicants and games of chance and (sacrificing to) stones set up and (dividing by) arrows are only uncleanliness, the devils work; so shun it that you may succeed." (5:90).

One of the reasons why the usage of drugs and alcohol is prohibited is because as a Muslim you are to pray five times a day. Remembrance and praise of God is a full time obligation of man so how can one fully praise God if his mind is clouded by the effects of intoxicants? When one is constantly thinking of God he is also remembering the laws God has laid down for him and thus his conduct towards other men and other creatures is of high moral standards because he knows that God is always watching. I doubt I need to remind you of all the social damage drugs, alcohol, and gambling has done to Western society. Certain groups of Arabs may have animosity against the West because of all the atrocious acts the Western governments have perpetrated against the Arab populace. Their only motive is the destruction of these Western nations. They rationalize their selling of drugs to the Western nations as a way of retaliation against them causing them social destruction. This is where they went wrong. Islam does not condone drug selling to Muslims or non-Muslims. The hatred in their hearts has driven them outside the boundaries of Islam thus committing this unlawful act. The ends are not justified by the means. The wrongdoing they fight against is only turned around and committed by them. Islam does not fight fire with fire but allows the cool waters of God to extinguish all the fires man has ignited.

If the Qur'an prohibits the usage of drugs and alcohol then common sense would also declare the prohibition of the sale of drugs and alcohol. Islam prohibits anything in excess because the only excessive thing you are meant to have is excessive obedience to the will of God. Excess of a physical thing leads you to wanting it more and more thus in time you will forget about the One True God and your only focus of worship will become that physical item. This is why addiction to any drug is so shattering to the user and those around him. The drug causes the user to worship the sensation of being high while at the same time it forces the seller to worship the money he receives for selling the drug. Soon both are worshipping false idols with no reward being received. Both minds are blinded to the fact of the One True God. This blindness is received by anyone who is doing something more often then praising God. Whether it is drugs, alcohol, sex, money, or power the greed for physical satisfaction leads to the idol worshiping of material goods forgetting about the only being that deserves praise and worship, the One True God.

All of God's creatures whether animate or inanimate are due respect, kindness, mercy, generosity, pity, and forgiveness by Muslims. These and many other virtues that are taught in the faith of Islam are to be used in regards to all of God's creatures, non-Muslim and Muslims alike. There is not one code of morality towards Muslims and a different one for non-Muslims. All men are created equal and are to be treated equally. Any straying from this practice is strongly forbidden. Any verse in the Qur'an that talks about fighting or killing the disbelievers was sent for one reason alone. These verses were revealed during times of persecution from the Meccan pagan tribes. The early Muslims were given permission to fight their enemies only as a way of protecting the message of Islam. God gave permission to fight the disbelievers only after the early Muslims had endured torture, persecution, and murder at the hands of the idol worshipping Meccans for many many years. These verses were revealed as a way of God giving permission to His Prophet to take up arms in protection of the weak small band of Muslims.

This taking up of arms was meant for the protection of the religion not for the gain of wealth or land as in much of European history. These verses in no way allow or promote the killing that so many misguided Arabs have committed. These verses were revealed for a certain time in Islamic history not for any man to use at his own disposal. The Constitution of the United States gave men the right to bear arms to fight and kill the British. If the Constitution made up by a couple of weak men can give men the right to fight and kill the enemy who dares to think that they should question God for giving men the right to fight in defense of His faith?

Many Western and Christian writers have adopted the use of the word infidel. The noun form infidel comes from the adjective infidelity meaning immoral. The Arabs used this adjective to label the Christians during the Crusades because of their wrongful ways. This noun cannot be used to mean all Christians because there are many Christians who are very righteous and commit highly moral acts. This adjective infidel can be used to describe acts committed by many men of different faiths, races, and ways of life. The anti-Islam propaganda machine has taken the opportunity to promote the hate of Islam more by making all Muslims out as enemies against Western societies. The propaganda authors are the ones who have convinced the Western nations that they are the "infidels" but do they know all the Christians of the world? Their lumping all Christians and Westerners under one group is just as bad as saying all Muslims are terrorists. Prejudice and discrimination against a group of people is unlawful in Islam no matter if the group is Muslim or Non Muslim.

Why should the East bow down to the West? Would the West bow down to the East? Should women bow to men? The old to the young? The Black to the White? When will man understand that all bowing should be done before the Almighty, the One True God Himself? This act of man bowing to man is idolatry in its highest form. When will man destroy the selfishness that deceives him to shed the blood of his brother? This physical worship of the flesh has destroyed man throughout time and will only help to bring his tribe closer and closer to destruction. This hatred that has been instilled in the people of today will only consume and destroy him. By putting himself on a pedestal of greatness above the other cultures and faiths of the world he has painted himself as the supreme ruler. What a terrible sin!

The most terrible thing a man can do in the eyes of God is the worshiping of false idols. This sin is so wrong because it takes away the obedience and praise that only the One True God deserves. Secondly it makes dealing with other men unfair and unequal. No man who thinks he is a god can equally respect his fellow man thus resulting in war and violence because he thinks all power and greatness belongs to him. Only through praising the One True God will mankind be able to find a respectful union with his fellow man. If you don't respect God do you think you can respect your neighbor? The Holy Qur'an, the revealed scripture of the Islamic faith, contains many laws and commandments given by God for the purpose of helping man to grow. In the Qur'an God tells man that He has given man two different kinds of laws: Laws that have definite unarguable meanings and laws that are left open for man to interpret through his own wisdom. Although many of these laws are left open to interpretation, they must not go against any of those definite laws of God. These laws that God has given man the power to interpret must coincide and follow the rules of conduct, justice, and morality that God has given. These laws must follow the rules of common sense and logic that God has also put in place for the benefit of mankind.

The law of the Sharia is used in many predominantly Muslim countries. These laws consist of the many laws found in the Qur'an yet many of the laws in the Qur'an are left up to man for interpretation. Since man is not a perfect creature, he is prone to make errors in judgment. This means that even a law found in the Sharia could contain an error in judgment because no man is perfect, a fact that no man can hide from. Through God's wisdom He gives the world the proof that even though man has received a perfect faith, man himself will never be perfect leaving God Himself the only Perfect being in the universe. How Great is God's wisdom!

Even though many Western writers say that the Sharia tells Muslims to commit all sorts of atrocities you must realize that many of the things included in these laws are only the input of a weak, misguided, and mortal men. The truthfulness of these laws must not go against the defined laws of the Qur'an to be deemed legit and of pure Islam. Man in his weak state of mind cannot overpower the laws of God. Only by following the laws of God will the light of the True Islam shine through. Only by seeing who finishes the race will you see who is truly correct. Lies cannot outlast the truth. Remember the Qur'an was revealed to preserve life and to help it grow not to see it mutilated, tortured, and killed for all nations of men and women.

Since no man is allowed to force his way of life on another man Islam teaches that if a man says he is a Muslim no other man is to say he is not. Only God has the right to judge mankind and too say who is Muslim or not. The Qur'an states:

"Surely Allah enjoins justice and the doing of good (to others) and the giving to the kindred, and He forbids indecency and evil and rebellion. He admonishes you that you may be mindful." (16:90).

This verse deals with the different degrees of goodness and evil. The lowest form of goodness is returning good for good. The next stage is the doing of good where one receives no benefit. The highest stage is that in which one's nature is so inclined to do good that he has not to make an effort for doing good; he does good to all people like one who does for his own kindred. This verse also deals with the levels of evil doing. From the smallest infraction to the wrongful acts which violate the rights of individuals and nations. Just by going into the Qur'an all of man's questions can be answered and explained.

One of the most horrible practices known throughout the history of mankind is slavery. Slavery based on racial background, financial indebtedness, or through war has been practiced by many groups through out the centuries. Yet one religion has been given to man to finally end this practice. Islam is that way of life. Many tribes practiced this institution so in order for God to give this message to stop slavery the message has to be able to apply to all the tribes of the earth. That is one of the beauties of Islam. Its message is the universal solution for all of man's problems. Many people rationalize the institution of slavery as being synonymous with hatred although hatred isn't even the proper word to use. There was no anger between the European and the Africans they enslaved. The thing about it was that they perceived the Africans as not even human beings worthy of expressing basic human emotions lowering them below the status of animals. The Europeans looked upon the Africans as one looks upon a horse, cow, or other animal of labor. But the Africans walked upright on two legs like the Europeans and had towns and villages like the Europeans. The Africans had laws and treaties just like the Europeans. What was it that allowed the Europeans to perceive the Africans as less then human almost animal?

The European version of Christianity allowed and condoned the enslaving of the Africans. What I mean by European version of Christianity is that Jesus Christ himself never condoned the practice of slavery because his people were enslaved for hundreds of years and he knew of the damage it could cause against humanity. The only people that could have condoned slavery had to have been a people who were never enslaved yet had always been the masters. The European church from its beginning always had power and control. Whether politically, financially, or militarily it has always had power in the Western world. Only an organization of this much clout and power could have rationalized such a practice the terrible magnitude as slavery. That is exactly what happened. Yes, let me say it again it was the European church that takes the credit for embarking on the practice of slavery.

Let me tell you the story. A European explorer had come across the country of Africa. After being amazed by seeing such dark people as the Africans his amazement sparked his greed. He captured one of the Black Africans and brought him back to Europe. He brought the kidnapped African before the church and told them of a scheme he had made up in his mind. He told the church of how un-European like the dark skinned African was and how the number of Africans was countless and that by enslaving them to sell to the Europeans the profit to be made was limitless. The power of greed overtook the church when they saw the dollar signs as the explorer hatched his scheme. Yet the church knew they might run into some opposition so they thought of a plan to be able to rationalize the enslaving of the Africans.

After searching long and hard they found their solution through the story of the Bible. Yes, I said the Bible. The story they found comes from the Old Testament. The story is about a Prophet of God who had a son. The son of the Prophet had a grandson named Ham. One such evening the Prophet was said to have gotten drunk and he commenced to take off all his clothes. The son of the prophet is then reported to have walked in on his father and he proceeded to see his father naked. For this act of sin God was supposed to have cursed the Prophet and his son, but the punishment was not to be inflicted on the Prophet or even his son but on his innocent grandson Ham. This curse upon Ham was that all of his descendants till the end of time must bow down and serve the rest of mankind. This is where the European church found their excuse to rationalize the enslaving of the Africans. After reading the story of Ham the Church declared the

Africans the so-called descendants of Ham without having any knowledge of the ancestry of the African race. They rationalized this story to mean that the Africans were meant to be enslaved because of God's curse and that it was the European race they were meant to bow down and serve. Since the church was paid a hefty tax for all sales the selling of slaves would boost the income of the church million fold. They saw the opportunity to make a buck and they took it. It was nothing personal against the Africans but was only the greed of the European church. They had the power to do whatever they pleased whether moral or immoral.

These enslavers should not be hated but we should feel sorry for their plight due to the misguidance of their leaders. I truly forgive those misguided European people for their enslaving of my ancestors. The greed of the European people for wealth was the only motivation for the enslavement of the Africans and their country. The church also saw this enslavement as a way of turning these "savages" into good-hearted kind Christians just like them. What a lie. Many of the European slave ships were named after good Christian saints with one slave ship being named "The Jesus Christ." Yes, a ship that carried thousands of innocent Africans to their deaths was named "The Jesus Christ." Is that the high moral example of European Christian dignity and human rights that so many Western Christian writers talk about originating in the West? Do the research and you will see that what I say is the truth. This is the history of those men who claim today to be the torch holders of freedom and human rights in the world today. This torch was not lit then and it is definitely not lit today. The governments of the West have blinded you from the truth today just as the Church was blinded by greed.

The Prophet Muhammad (saw) denounced slavery according to the teachings of Islam making one of the first and most important tenants of Islam the destruction of the institution of slavery. The revelation of the Qur'an gave immediate and simple laws concerning the end of slavery. By reading the Qur'an one finds that God Himself told man to stop the practice of slavery. The Holy Prophet urged his companions to release all their slaves under the threat of angering God. The basic rights of equality found in Islam give no man the right to own, control, or manipulate the thoughts or actions of any man, women, or child. Islam gives all humans the right to make their own decision regarding their thoughts and actions.

Many Christian and Western writers accuse the Qur'an of accepting slavery. Those ignorant misguided people say that the Qur'an says to own slaves yet they cannot show a single verse that condones the practice of slavery. They cannot show one verse that says the Prophet should own slaves yet they use these lies to misguide you readers whose knowledge of the Qur'an and Islam is less then theirs. Look into the Qur'an and you will find no mention of condoning the practice of slavery. Before the revelation of the Qur'an slavery was practiced. The only way that the Qur'an discusses slavery is how one should free his slaves.

No religion has laid so much stress on the upliftment of the poor and distressed as Islam and it is the only religion that enjoins the granting of freedom to slaves. The Holy Prophet (saw) is the only bringer of a religion who showed the noble example of freeing all slaves that he ever had and helping in the freedom of others both spiritually and physically.

To say the Qur'an is merciless is mere lies. Every other book that exists in revealed religions was revealed to a certain group of men. Isn't it strange that none of these books that exist today were revealed to the Europeans? Where is the mercy for the Europeans of the world? The Qur'an is that mercy. The Qur'an is the only book that claims to be for the entire human race. The Qur'an was revealed for the Europeans and all ethnicities. As long as people continue to follow a faith that was given to another people they will never be free to find their own freedom, destiny, and truths. They have become enslaved to the people whose lies they follow so blindly. All men were meant to worship the One True God and only through a faith that teaches unity will they be able to find true freedom.

It is hard to recognize true dignity in Christianity. Is it Christian or European dignity? This is the problem with Christianity. In many Modern Christian churches, there is a picture of a very Anglo looking man who is suppose to represent Jesus. However, most people would admit that this is not a likely representation of what he would look like since his ancestry is Middle Eastern. What reward would a Black man possess by bowing down to a White god. What vast questions of inferiority would arise in the minds of its Black followers? Would an all White church have a picture of a Black Jesus hanging above its alter? This is the beauty of Islam. Since its description of God is colorless and sexless it gives men and women of all tribes and colors the dignity to be able to become godlike in character because they are basing the quality and character of God on his attributes rather then his color or sex.

This same quality also dignifies women in that they also can be able to try to become as righteous as possible. Can a woman who is proud of her sex ever be able to achieve complete mental freedom as long as she is still bowing down to a man? This whole concept of a European god is designed to keep the European man enslaved to the thought that the European man is superior and is a god. Isn't it strange that while the European race makes up less then one fourth of the world's population Christianity is the largest religion in the world with all of these people worshiping a picture of an European man. Christianity not only destroys the dignity of the colored races of the world it also crushes the dignity of the female species. Where is the love there?

"The adulteress and the adulterer, flog each of them (with) a hundred stripes, and let not pity for them detain you from obedience to Allah, if you believe in Allah And the Last Day, and let a party of believers witness their chastisement." (24:2).

Chastity as a virtue is not given the first place in modern Western society hence adultery is not considered a sufficiently serious offense to subject the guilty party to any punishment. This breach of trust ruins families, destroys household peace, and deprives innocent children of their equal parental affection. In the West adultery is not looked upon as seriously as the breach of trust of a few dollars. This is why Islamic laws seems so severe to Westerners. The usage of stoning is prohibited since nowhere in the Qur'an does it speak of stoning as a punishment for any crime. The use of flogging is to be used as a tool to disgrace the culprit rather than to torture the culprit. During the time of the Prophet (saw) the whip was not used rather a stick or a shoe. The culprit was not stripped naked in order to give the culprit the ability to not be harmed physically. Mental embarrassment is the purpose of this punishment. Only extreme situations require extreme punishment in Islam. One of the main tenants in Islam is justice. The Qur'an teaches equality and fairness in all aspects of life. It teaches equality in rewards as well as in punishments. All punishments in Islam are to be equal to the crime committed whether it is a social or individual crime. God through His great and infinite wisdom has given man the prescribed punishments for crimes but He has also given man the qualities of fairness and logic to build a society based on forgiveness and mercy. God gives us many examples of mercy through His own acts and expects us to follow His lead.

JESUS AND ISLAM

What has the Western world accomplished that it feels that it should be able to dictate the difference between right and wrong in the world? This is their desire to control the thoughts and actions of all of mankind. Simply because it has enslaved its own people it thinks it has the right to poison the rest of the world as well. All the technology that it has today was just as groundbreaking as the technology of the past during its climax. The same military might it claims today was the same military might it boasted generations ago. The same wealth and political prowess it claims to have modernized into the greatest on earth is the same as that of the empires of ancient Europe.

But where are these great European empires that existed in the past? Where are these mighty armies that once boasted great military victories? Can you dare to think that one day the United States will one day be listed among these fallen empires along with Britain and Rome? What was it that caused the demise of these great kingdoms? Will that same plague be cast upon the continent of North America bringing it to its knees as well? Do you wish to wait around and wait for this destruction or do you wish to avoid its torment?

The West cannot impact Islam because Islam will never reach this destiny of destruction that the Western world is spiraling towards. Only through True Islam will the West avoid such pain. Islam taught man over a century ago the many qualities and guidelines that the West is just recently starting to incorporate in its societies. Islam is the pie that the West chooses to take small bites of to satisfying their desire for truth and freedom. Yet the bites they take are only to appease the few who demand more. These will not be enough to ever free them from the torment and pain they are getting closer to every day.

In Islam Jesus is revered as a prophet of God sent to his people, the Jews to revive the teachings of the prophets before him. Many Christians say Jesus is the prototype of king in the West but that couldn't be any farther from the truth. Christ was not a European. How many non-European Kings were there in the history of Europe? Christ was a carpenter. How many kings of Europe ever dirtied their hands with the laborious work of the common folk? Christ was a poor man with barely the rags to cover his body. How many kings of Europe covered their body with the coarse wool of the serfs under them instead of the fine robes of silk and linen accustomed to royalty? Christ was a poor man who preached to give all your worldly possessions away to God's cause. How many European kings gave away all their riches to God and his fellow man out of love for his Creator? Christ taught to turn the other cheek when insulted or struck. How many European kings turned away from war when violated by another country or foe? The arrogance of the Western kings boasted no similarity to humbleness of Christ. To boast these similarities is to lie out of mere jealousy of the virtuous and moral characteristics of Christ.

Jesus is often referred to as the Prince of Peace. A prince of his own people maybe but a White prince I say not. A bringer of peace and truth for his own people but for any other race I say not. Christ wasted no time in stating that his mission was only for his own people and that he cared not for the troubles of others especially the Whites of that time. Jesus was a Jew. Jesus was sent to his people to deliver a message that was only meant for them and could only cure their misguidings. This message would have done nothing for the Westerners as they had no knowledge of prior information that Christ only came to reiterate and ask his people to follow again. God put compassion into the hearts of Christ's followers because of the immense love and dedication that Christ had for God and the message he was to give to his people. The beauty of Christ shown like a bright light for his people but this light was closed to those outside the door of his race. Yes, Jesus is a fine example as a man and a leader but his message and usefulness was limited only to the ranks and problems of his own people. This compassion was instilled only because his people were led so far astray that the only thing that could bring them back to the truth of their faith was overwhelming belief and love for the message and the message bearer. Christ said, "I am the way, the truth, and the light." He meant that by following His message his people could find the truth and prosperity they were looking for. His people were not the Romans nor are they those of European decent today.

Since modern Christianity teaches the worship of a man this ideology allows the reproduction of other false idols. A lie cannot support itself so it must rely on other untruths to keep it alive or it will crumble under the weight of the truth. The worship of Christ has led to the worship of country and flag. This country is all about physical gain so it has ultimately led to the worship of money. Even when one has tried the other forms of worship and they all have failed him he can even try the faith of worshiping his own skin, also known as fascism. The people of the West have continued to worship one form or another of one of these faiths yet none of them will be able to pull them away from the fire they draw nearer to every day. All the ways that cover the eyes of the West can be traced back to idolatry. These false gods have corrupted and disillusioned many cultures who seek the same foolish desires leading them all to receive the same fate.

The European version of Christianity was never meant to promote anything but the idea of salvation through the blood of Christ. The only purpose it has ever served was to give people a false sense of being saved and freed through Christ's supposed resurrection. Modern Christianity is a conclusion without performing the experiment or receiving the paycheck without ever performing any work. Modern Christianity is getting dessert without eating your brussel sprouts. Is this what happens in the real world? Christianity does not teach according to the laws of logic and rationality. It may reiterate morals and guidelines from other faiths but by itself teaches no laws or guidelines that men can use today to improve their everyday lives. How can a faith like that cure the many problems faced by people today? It can't. As long as you wait for a man to come back from the dead your mind will be so anxiously awaiting his arrival that you will never be able to see that the solution to your problems has come and that the longer you wait the problems you have will only get worse. Take for example one of the worst problems of the Western world, alcoholism. What does the Bible say about alcohol and how does it recommend curing this social plague? Teenage pregnancy is on the rise. How does the Bible recommend stopping this epidemic? A failing education system. How does the Bible recommend saving it and those drowning in its murky waters? All of these and many more of today's social ailments were given cures 1,500 years ago in the Qur'an.

Answers to the problems that exist in the Western world were not discussed in his teachings because these problems did not exist within the people Christ was sent to help. Unfortunately, many if not all of the problems that Jesus did discuss in his teachings, i.e. gambling, are still prevalent today if not more so. Only the Qur'an can completely help people of the West because the Qur'an addresses problems for all time and all people. The Qur'an is the universal answer. If Islam can cure and free the wild tribes of Arabia and turn them into dedicated followers of the One True God it can also free and enlighten the people of the West.

Numerous times in the Qur'an the word righteous is used to describe the best of those in the sight of God. Whoever practices their faith to the best of their ability and strives in good deeds will attain paradise. In the Qur'an God talks of the fate of the disbelievers since they are his creatures He and only He has the right to judge them and their actions. No man has the right to say if one man is better or whether he is Muslim or not. Man is judged by God concerning his actions and will receive his due reward in this life as well as the next. In Islam a

Christian has the right to obtain heaven based on his deeds just as well as a Muslim. A Muslim can receive punishment just as a Christian so he needs not to physically respond to the actions and words of disbelievers because only God has the power and authority to punish whom He pleases.

"Muhammad is the Messenger of Allah, and those with him are firm of heart against the disbelievers, compassionate among themselves. Thou seest them bowing down, prostrating themselves, seeking Allah's grace and pleasure. Their marks are on their faces in consequence of prostration. That is their description in the Torah-and their description in the Gospel-like seed–produce that puts forth its sprouts, then strengthens it, so it becomes stout and stands firmly on its stem, delighting the sowers that He may enrage the disbelievers on account of them. Allah has promised such of them as believe and do good, forgiveness and a great reward." (48:29).

The Arabic word which means firm also means brave and firm of heart. The translation used by Western authors as fierce or vehement is not correct. The Muslims stood firm against the disbelievers but they were never fierce or harsh in the treatment of the non-Muslims. A Muslim is taught to remain firm in his beliefs and in his actions because the ways of the disbelievers can lead the Muslims to feelings of hatred and transgression. It is not wrong of a Christian to remain strong or firm of heart in his beliefs so why not a Muslim? The disbelievers are those that do not believe in God. This verse demonstrates that any Jew, Muslim, or Christian that practices his or her faith and does good deeds can achieve paridise. The ways of the disbelievers are always aimed at destroying the truth. The righteous must always be on their guard against the devious ways of the deceivers.

PROTECTOR OF WOMEN

The Qur'an explains thoroughly the institution of the veil. The veiling of women is not something invented by Islam. Remember that Islam is the perfection of all the faiths so nine out of ten times the same tenants that are found in Islam are also found in other ways of life. The previous revealed books also contain traces of similar teachings and Islam only perfects their usefulness. The revealed religions teach women to be modest in clothes and action. The Bible teaches that modesty and reverence demanded the veiling of the face and that ladies of high moral rank used the veil. In the following passage of the Old Testament we read about what Rebekah did before Isaac:

"When Rebekah raised her eyes, she caught sight of Isaac and swung herself down off the camel. Then she said to the servant 'who is that walking in the field to meet us?' and the servant said 'It is my master' and she proceeded to take a head cloth and to cover herself." (Genesis 24:64,65).

In the New Testament we also read:

"But every woman that prays or prophesies with her head uncovered shames her head for it is one and the same as if she were (woman) with a shaved head. For if a woman does not cover herself let her also be shorn; but if it is disgraceful for a woman to be shorn or shaved, let her be covered." (1 Corinthian 11:5,6).

It is obvious that the both sections of the Bible regard the veiling of women as a pious act. The fact remains that Islam has given women rights which have no equal in any other religion or society. The veil is far from a burden on women it is a blessing for them. The Holy Qur'an has preserved the teachings of Islam in its purest form, prescribes the correct commandments, explains the reasons and wisdom behind them, and also points out the benefits which can be gained by following them. The Qur'an states:

"And say to the believing women that they restrain their looks and guard their private parts and that they display not their beauty or their embellishment except that which is apparent thereof, and that they draw their head coverings over their bosoms, and that they display not their beauty or their embellishment save to their husbands, or to their fathers, or the fathers of their husbands, or their sons, or their sons of their husbands, or their brothers, or the sons of their brothers, or their sons of their sisters, or

women who are their companions, or those whom their right hands posses, or such of male attendants as have no desire for women, or young children who have not attained knowledge of the hidden parts of women. And that they strike not their feet so that what hide of their ornaments may become known. And turn ye to Allah all together, O believers that you may prosper." (24:32).

This verse directs the believing women to restrain their eyes when they happen to face men, to guard their chastity, and not to display their beauty whether it is natural or artificial. The believing men have also been given a similar commandment from God in the following verse:

"Say to the believing men that they restrain their looks and guard their private parts. That is purer for them. Surely Allah is well aware of what they do." (24:31).

"It is perfectly clear that both men and women share equally the responsibility of observing this commandment. They should both observe the "veil" of the eyes. God never gives orders to His servants without reason yet through great wisdom. Commentary on these verses has been given. It should be kept in mind that the natural condition of man, which is the source of his passion, is that he cannot depart from it without a complete change in himself. His passions are bound to be roused and put in peril when they are confronted with the occasion and opportunity for indulging in this vice. God Almighty has not instructed us that we might freely gaze at women outside the prohibited degree and contemplate their beauty and observe all their movements in dancing etc. He has instructed that we should do so with pure looks. Nor have we been instructed to listen to the singing of these women and to lend ear to tales of their beauty, but that we should do so with pure intent. We have been positively commanded not to look at their beauty, whether with pure intent or otherwise, nor to listen to their musical voices or descriptions of their good looks, whether with pure intent or otherwise. We have been directed to eschew all this as we eschew carrion, so that we should not stumble. It is almost certain that our free glances would cause the other or us to stumble sometime.

God Almighty desires that our eyes and our hearts and all our limbs and organs should continue in a state of purity, He has furnished us with this excellent teaching. There can be no doubt that unrestrained looks become a source of danger. If we placed soft bread before a hungry dog it would be vain to hope that the dog should pay no attention to it. Thus God Almighty desired that human faculties should not be provided with any occasion for secret functioning and should not be confronted with anything that might incite dangerous tendencies.

This is the philosophy that underlines Islamic regulations relating to the observance of the veil. The Book of God does not aim at keeping women in seclusion like prisoners. This is the concept of those who are not acquainted with the correct pattern of Islamic ways. The purpose of these regulations is to restrain men and women from letting their eyes to rove freely and from displaying their good looks and beauties, for therein lies the good of both men and women. It should be remembered that to restrain ones looks and to direct them only towards observing that which is permissible is described in Arabic by the expression "ghadde basar" which is the expression employed in the Holy Qur'an in this context. It does not behoove a pious person who desires to keep his heart pure that he should lift his eyes freely in every direction like an animal. It is necessary that such a one should cultivate the habit of "ghadde basar" in his social life. This is a blessed habit through which his natural impulses would be converted into high moral qualities without interfering with his social needs.

This is the quality that is called chastity in Islam. We can understand the wisdom behind the teachings of Islam concerning the veil and the spiritual benefits which both men and women can gain if they follow them. It is also clear that observing the veil is not a duty for women alone but for both the sexes. God has prescribed these commandments to the believing men and believing women separately so there must be great wisdom behind this also. One of the obvious reasons behind this is to point out clearly that each of them is responsible for his or her own behavior when carrying out and obeying these injunctions. This proves that the Muslim man has nothing to do with forcing the women to obey his order, out of any love for domination on his side.

Women are by nature the delicate sex and they need special care and protection. Thus Islam treats women as precious treasures that should be guarded and protected from being startled or molested by people in any way. Islam is protecting the inner feelings of women concerning how they feel about their physical appearance through the usage of the veil. Let us take a second to examine the roles of men and women in society. Man is physically stronger and that is why his role is to go out and provide for the family. He is the protector of the family from danger. But this does not degrade the position of the woman. If the need or desire arises she may work outside the home. She with her loving and caring nature is responsible of looking after the members of the family. She is the protector against the internal dangers. She is responsible for the moral education of the children. The combined efforts of the man and woman produce the perfect family. The protection provided by the man does not mean they are superior over women, but it emphasizes the importance of the role of women in society. Women need to be protected from outside dangers so that they can give full attention to carrying out their sacred duties.

The Islamic veil symbolizes the spiritual protection of the Muslims. As the woman represents the spiritual body of the Islamic society, this veil takes a palpable form in the case of women while it remains intangible in the case of men. Women need protection from external dangers and this is why their veil is physical because it represents physical protection while for men the veil is concealed because it represents their internal protection. But must always be reminded that observing the veil is an obligation for both sexes even if it assumes different forms. Not only does it protect from external influences, it also protects a woman from vanity, self-consciousness, and other internal conflict.

The Islamic veil enjoins both men and women to cover themselves with the garment of righteousness described by God as the best garment. This means that the covering of the body signifies the covering of the nakedness of the soul and its protection from evil by becoming righteous in action, word, and thought: The ultimate goal of a believer. The Islamic veil of a woman is a symbol of her protection from the external dangers that can effect her moral and spiritual advancement. The real Islamic veil is more than a covering of the physical body. It implies also the drawing of a virtual curtain upon herself to protect her from all evil surroundings. As a reward for her great service to humanity, God Himself encompasses her and protects her with His mercy. Her outer garment is a symbol of this protection and mercy. Her outer garment is a proclamation to the world that she is under the protection of the Lord of the Universe and that nobody should dare cause her any inconvenience or harm without incurring His wrath.

In the Western society women have neglected their duties as wives and mothers and have begun to compete with men in all fields of life. Women are freely mixing with men fighting with one another to attract men. They find false pleasure in exposing their beauty and competing in displaying their beauty in contests. They are degrading their bodies as if they are a product available for display and sale. They are not aware of the acts of harm and injury they are causing themselves and their society.

Is this really freedom? What was thought to be freedom turned out to be the very cause of her degradation and the destruction of her dignity and far from acquiring her freedom. She has been reduced to the degree of slavery at the disposal of men. It has become socially accepted and expected that women will spend excessive amounts of money and time on her hair, make-up, and nails. For what? These are nothing but a superficial vanity. We are bombarded on a daily basis with half naked woman in the media implying to woman of the West that all female's bodies should look like these leading to eating disorders. Women are killing themselves to fit some pre-conceived notion of beauty. Females are taught from a very young age if not explicitly, then it is implied, that if they are unable to attract a man based on their physical attributes alone that they are of less worth. Again I ask you, is this really freedom?

The Barbie doll is often used as a role model for young females in the West. Barbie is a blinding lie. What does Barbie contribute to society? What does she do to make society a more moral place? How does it bring one closer to God? Since I haven't found any positive things let's look at the negative. Since Barbie is the ideal object of beauty then anyone that does not look like her must be ugly right? How does a girl feel about herself if her weight is not proportioned to the weight of this plastic doll? This doll is only meant to promote the fact that blonde hair and blue eyes are the only things beautiful in the world. This shows the fact that if its user is not White, blond, and skinny she is worth nothing. The worship of physical characteristics is nothing more than the worship of a man. Thanks Christianity. With its barely clothed dolls Barbie is nothing more than an idol that young girls worship and try their hardest to be like. This often results in girls hating the way they look because their waist is not as small or their skin is not as clear often resulting in girls becoming physically and mentally traumatized. Only Islam gives females the tools to protect themselves from this terrible abuse.

If we look at the "free" Western societies of today we will find no trace of morality, let alone spirituality. Broken marriages, illegitimate children, abortion, adultery, are only a few of the problem in this and other Western nations. The easy availability of women for the pleasure of men has resulted in women no longer desired by men and therefore we see more evils like child abuse, homosexuality, drug addiction, crimes of rape, and murder for sexual excitement. It is clearly seen that the ones who are first to suffer are women yet it is them alone who bear the majority of responsibility of allowing this to happen.

The Holy Qur'an warned women of these problem 1,500 years ago. This is why God has put more responsibility on women than men in this respect for it is women who will suffer more. The Islamic veil honors women and frees them from the obstacles that prevent her moral and spiritual advancement and thus it is the means of her deliverance from the sufferings and ills she faces in today's society.

When women in the world today can understand the real implications of the true teachings of Islam concerning the veil and if they would know of the benefits they can gain and the high stations they can attain they will soon want their freedom from societal ills. They would be fighting to wear the veil where they could secure their true freedom and find true and real peace and tranquility both mentally and physically. In the veil lies true honor and dignity.

It is very easy to see the influence of idolitry in today's Western culture. Modern idolitry is a faith based on misguidance. Therefore it is safe to say that anything that falls under the umbrella of idolitry can be considered to be tainted with some form of misinformation and misguidance. How does one go about finding which information is legit and helpful to the cause of man's spiritual upliftment and which information will help cause mankind's physical and moral downfall. This labyrinth of information has only caused the Western world to wander aimlessly through out time and land only to find all the passageways to the truth blocked and barricaded by lies. Each time a door is slammed shut in the face of these lost helpless travelers they become more and more distant from the One True God, their only help out of this destructive maze.

The Western worlds' treatment of women is no different. The leaders of the West know that the feminist rights movement will never give woman the rights they are fighting for and that the more women fight for equality with men the more they will loose their femininity. Instead of striving to be equal with men they are only trying to become men discarding all the beauties and good things that make a women special. In the end they are only destroying their inner beauty to try to satisfy the men they are trying to be equal to. The more they try to be like men the more they loose of their pride, freedom, and beauty. The more they struggle to get closer to men and his false freedoms the farther they get from God and His blessed plans.

The rights of women against their husbands stated in the Qur'an are similar to those the husbands have against their wives. These statements must have caused quite a stir in a society that never valued the rights or even lives of women. Through this guidance women were now given an equal position to men, for they were declared to now have rights similar to those exercised against them. This declaration brought about a revolution in the whole world for the equality of the rights of women. Women's rights were never recognized by any previous reformer, prophet, or government leader thus establishing Muhammad (saw) as the pioneer of women's rights.

The Qur'an contains direction for the physical as well as the moral and spiritual welfare of man, and it deals with the most delicate of topics in the most delicate of language. Many of the phrases in the Qur'an dealing with the delicate questions relating to the sexes bring no shudder to the fairest of readers. The comparison of the woman to the tilth is simply to show that it is she who brings up the children and through whom is made the character of the man. This shows that the real object of sexual relations is not simply the satisfaction of carnal desires.

"Your wives are a tilth for you, so go in to your tilth when you like, and send (good) beforehand for yourselves. And keep your duty to Allah, and know that you will meet Him. And give good news to the believers." (2:223).

So many Western leaders, writers, and female rights groups try to use verses of the Holy Qur'an as anti-Islamic propaganda yet only continue to show their ignorance and misguidance. Female circumcision was never a concept of Islam. Furthermore it was never a concept of Arabia before the Prophet Muhammad (saw) let alone after his advent. Female circumcision was practiced throughout the continent of Africa in countries where Islam was never heard of. This is totally against the teachings of Islam. God teaches in the Holy Qur'an that no human being has the right to force another human being to do something against his own will. It is that simple. Anyone who forces something upon someone else is going against a direct order of God and Islam. Even if that person claims to be Muslim he is still in direct violation of God's commandments and will thus result in bringing about punishment from God. This practice of female circumcision is a complete violation against God because God created the female body to have the parts it does for a reason and a function.

To say you are doing something under the guise of Islam you must be able to prove it by showing it in the Holy Qur'an and since there is no mentioning of female mutilation of any kind in the Qur'an this practice of circumcision cannot be a practice of Islam. During times of Europe when females were forced to wear chastity belts was that ever considered a Christian practice? Remember that even though many peoples claim to be Muslim it doesn't mean that they have completely given up their tribal customs whether they are wrong or right. These tribal customs are not a part of True Islamic way of life and should not be confused with the faith of Islam or the freedom it offers.

Only the hatred of Islam forces people to write and spread lies against the beauty of Islam. They spread these lies for nothing but to hear their own voices. The beauty and truth of Islam will never be destroyed. Only the innocent minds they poison with their lies will suffer. Don't allow yourself to be infected by their greed and selfishness. If these lie mongers really respected and loved you they would tell you the truth so that you may succeed and grow. They only seek to keep you away from the beauty of Islam because without your praise they would be nothing. Will you continue to support their ignorance?

"Why did they not bring four witnesses of it? So, as they have not brought four witnesses, they are liars in the sight of Allah." (24:13).

The fact is that while the Qur'an takes a very serious view of the crimes against chastity, it also makes criminal the circulation of false reports affecting a woman's mental chastity. Thus even a lighter accusation in connection with misconduct is required the evidence of four witnesses. This clearly shows that Islam is deeply concerned with the physical status, emotional stability, and spiritual upliftment of women. The usage of slanderous lies and gossip not only hurts a woman's reputation but also damages her own self-esteem resulting in countless traumatic injuries. Ignorant people misquote this verse to think that verse to think that when a woman says she was raped she needs four witnesses to stand against the accused rapist, but that is totally wrong. Islam has covered all the bases to protect the rights of women and holds their self-esteem and security as a highest priority. The Holy Prophet (saw) is reported to have said, "Paradise lies at the feet of the Mother" and "Treat women like glass." These sayings showed how much compassion and care the Prophet (saw) had for the physical and mental well being of women.

No matter what word you put before kill Islam does not nor ever has condoned murder. No matter what the reason man may put to make murder sound glorious or needed it is unacceptable and illegal in the faith of Islam. For honor, religion, country, or faith murder is not permitted as a tool to bring about one's goals. The Qur'an does not contain a single verse that allows the crime of murder in any situation of an innocent person. Islam does not allow the murder of any person whether Muslim or non-Muslim. No man has the right to take another mans' life accept during a criminal proceeding where an organized court system uses fair and just laws to hand out the penalty of death for the crime it fits. Anyone who claims to be honor killing or killing for the cause of God is a fool and a liar. These misguided people will realize one day that it is only the wrath of God they will receive not His blessings.

The Qur'an often mentions the righteous women will be blessed with the fruits of paradise enforcing equality among the sexes. The same rights that are awarded men are given also to women. Although the physical duties of everyday life are different the in the eyes of God, for the betterment of society, the basic human rights are the same. In many verses of the Qur'an God Almighty reminds women that they share the equal reward as men in the hereafter. God often reminds women that the share of the reward they are due for the fulfillment of righteous deeds will not be a moment delayed.

Paradise is a place for faithful women as well as faithful men. The Qur'an also shows that paradise and its blessings are alike for men and women being not the least difference in this respect between the sexes. The Qur'an does not speak of any conjugal relations being maintained in a physical sense in the life to come moreover it has been shown on various occasions that where the blessings of paradise are spoken of these are nothing but physical manifestations of the spiritual blessings which the doers of good enjoy in this life too. The Holy Prophet (saw) constantly reminded his companions to show respect to their mothers, wives, daughters, and sisters. The Prophet (saw) is quoted as saying, "The most perfect of the believers in faith is the best of them in moral excellence, and the best of you are the kindest of you to their wives." In Islam the security of the female is regarded as a top priority since the responsibility of the raising of the children, according to the values of Islam, is such an important task while if not the most important.

RACE, RELIGION, AND LIES

When will these pitiful misguided souls ever find the truth? Let me explain their plight. The first thing we must do is separate religion from nationality. Christianity and Islam are religions. The words Arab and European denote nationality. Yet these Western authors continue to write as if Islam is something that can physically overcome a nationality of people. This is not possible. The only thing that Islam can change about a nationality is their way of life. Islam cannot remove the pigments in the genes of European people that make them White or remove the cells in your body that make your eyes blue or hair blonde. Islam does not wish to change you or your physical features but loves and respects them as God's beautiful creation.

What Islam is meant to do is just what it is meant to do to all the other races of the world. Islam was given to purify and free the heart, the mind, and the body of filth and immorality. That is the only goal and purpose of Islam. Islam is only here to help man grow and evolve into the perfect mirror of God's attributes. Islam is a filter that takes away all that is harmful to man and leaves him pure and healthy. Many people have started using filters in their home water and the bottled water sales have skyrocketed. Shouldn't the soul and mind also receive the same pleasure of cleanliness?

The only people that are scared of the coming of Islam to the West are those who profit and survive off of the evil and lies they promote in the Western world. They are criminals who prey on the weakness and misguidance of the Western people. These shepherds are really wolves who prey on the weak sheep of this wronged race. There is nothing to fear from Islam because it is your destiny and way out of this mental slavery that has been forced upon you for centuries. These criminals who plague your race trying to instill this hatred of Islam in you are only using your lack of knowledge for their own personal selfish gain. They use your lack of knowledge to destroy your chances of freedom from the evils of man and his inner greed. In the end they will only discard you and watch you crumble without lifting a hand to help. Islam is your only help.

I go back to the example of alcoholism. It was discussed earlier that the consumption of alcohol is prohibited in Islam. It is prohibited because like all intoxicants it impairs judgment leading to committing sins against others and oneself, i.e. fornication, drunken driving. It does not allow you to remember God and distinguish between right and wrong. But just think of how many people make so much money off the sales of alcohol. There are so many that I can only name a few: breweries, bottlers, farmers, scientists, ad agencies, the media, retailers, sports arenas, restaurants/bars, law enforcement, the list goes on and on. Each one of these then pays business, income, and sales taxes. So not only does the government earn money off state run liquor stores and off the sale of liquor licenses, but it also gets all of that tax revenue. Allowing even this one aspect of Islam to enter Western culture would be like shooting itself in the proverbial foot.

Contrary to what is currently practiced in many Middle Eastern countries, in the religion of Islam democracy takes on its true meaning. Under the Islamic life-style the word democracy is meant to describe a social environment where the voice of the masses is used to elect the government officials. Can we say that America is a true democracy? It is only the dollars of big businesses that fund the campaigns of elected officials not the voice of the average working man or woman. It is these companies that lobby for whom they want only to receive gov-ernment backing in the pursuit of the dollar. The people are the last to benefit from this immoral practice. We are told that we the people elect our president. Vote! Vote! Vote! We are told it is our right and privilege to be able to vote and choose our president. We are also told that Santa Claus drops presents down our chimney every Christmas but is that true also? What makes voting any different? In a country based on material wealth do you think that a country full of rich and powerful companies and people are going to allow the poor of this country to choose the person to govern this country? Would a parent allow the child to make the families decisions? If this were a true democracy, the popular would decide everything. However, the popular vote does not even elect a president. The Electoral College chooses the President not the civilian voters. Many under-stand this concept, however the majority of the average civilians do not. The con-cept of voting in America is only a lie to give Americans the illusion to think they have control over who is in charge. This lie is used only to keep people happy in thinking that they are free to control how this country is run. You are not in con-trol but are being controlled by those in power. If everyone voted for one candi-date the other candidate can still win if the Electoral College chooses him. Your vote does not matter.

It is only a drug given to you to make you believe that you count. Your gov-ernment has lied to you and the only way you will free yourself from their lies is through submission to the One True God not to the false ones they have in place now. Stand up and free yourself or continue to suffer under their lies and injustices. Islam accepts pure democracy, but the corrupted form of democracy that exists in the United States is not lawful. In the U.S., the corporations with the deepest pockets buy votes. Companies endorse whom they want thus presidents are bought like milk at a supermarket. The winning candidate is not chosen for what he can do for the people but what he will do for the huge corporations. Is this democracy beneficial to the people or to the CEO's? Islam teaches fair dealings and this is not fair by a long shot.

To say that the Muslims were never persecuted only shows one's lack of knowledge and lack of common sense. Never has a Prophet not been persecuted by the people to whom he was sent to reform. Never has a group of righteous people living among wrongdoers not been persecuted. This persecution occurred not only because the people in power were committing acts of immorality and worshiping false idols, but also because they felt their authority being threatened by the new leader. This was no different for Muhammad (saw). His own uncle despised and fought against him and his followers were abused with the utmost of cruelties. Muslims were buried in the sand up to their necks and stoned to death. The slaves who converted to Islam were beaten and killed. Muslims were laid out in the sun with large rocks laid on their chest just because they worshiped the God of Muhammad (saw). Muslims arms and legs were tied to separate camels and their bodies were ripped into pieces as the camels ran in opposite directions. All of this because they chose the One True God over the many false idols of pagan Mecca.

Colonialism is the politically correct word for conquer. Politically correct means to lie to make it sound good when it is really bad. Is a lie good? They say that history is written by the victors. Colonialism is the politically correct way of stating when the European nations conquered the continent of North America by killing millions of its inhabitants. A land cannot be colonized when it is already inhabited by another group of people. This is another lie of Western authors and leaders. To say that European countries colonized North America they only insult the Americans who already for generations had established law-bearing societies with civilized treaties, governments, and codes of living. This is what European governments have done to countless other countries and races all under the lie of Western colonialism. Who gave the Western governments the authority to say who is civilized or not?

Islam is a code of living designed by God to be able to exist in any form of government designed by man. All of man's laws originate from laws of God so since Islam is God's law perfected then the faith of Islam must be able to exist under man's laws. Islam is based on morality; the doing of good deeds, so why would any country not want to have citizens who only do good deeds? Wouldn't you like to live in a neighborhood of people who only do good things? Wouldn't you want your child going to school with other children who are as respectful and as kind as yours? I would.

RELATIONSHIPS OUTSIDE OF ISLAM

The Qur'an clearly explains that there is no punishment for apostasy and blasphemy to be dealt by the hands of Muslims. The fair name of Islam has been darkened by murderous directives issued against writers who continue writing blasphemous remarks about the Prophet of God and the Qur'an. No matter what these remarks say there is no such penalty of death prescribed in Islam for this offense. None at all. No such instructions are contained in any verse of the Holy Qur'an. Let it also be noted that no one demanding these assassinations has quoted a single verse from the Holy Qur'an recommending this penalty.

No Prophet was more blasphemed, maligned, insulted, and abused during his lifetime than the Prophet Muhammad (saw). He and his followers were subjected to every verbal and physical harassment. He was forced to migrate from his birthplace to escape the severe torture. Ten years later he returned at the head of ten thousand followers, yet he forgave his persecutors for their cruel acts. This was the attitude of the Seal of the Prophets (saw) and thus the attitude that all Muslims should try to follow and duplicate today. Many misguided voices say that apostates from Islam should be met with death, but in fact there is not a single verse in the 114 chapters of the Qur'an that prescribe this fate for renouncing the faith of Islam. The Qur'an states:

"Those who believe, then disbelieve, then again believe, then disbelieve, and then increase in disbelief, Allah will never forgive them nor will He guide them to the right way." (4:138).

This verse clearly shows that any man has the right to enter and re enter Islam if he chooses. It is not up to any man to say who is a Muslim or not. This verse clearly shows that no man has the right to physically punish anyone who leaves the faith of Islam. Were death the punishment for one who leaves Islam then there arises no question of having the opportunity of accepting Islam again. This verse clearly mentions apostates who again accept Islam. There is no mention in the Holy Qur'an or teaching of the Prophet Muhammad (saw) of any punishment for an apostate to be handed out by another man. The punishment for this act is solely to be handed out by God. Man is free to accept or reject whatever faith he chooses. God says in the Holy Qur'an in the most simplest and easy to understand language:

"There is no compulsion in religion." (2:257).

"It is the truth from your Lord; wherefore let him who will, disbelieve." (18:30).

Could this commandment be any plainer? Western writers try deceive their readers by saying that Islam directs death upon any Muslim who leaves Islam yet their lies are merely their own words offering no verses of the Qur'an to back up their malicious statements. Islam recognizes and promotes the right of freedom of conscious and belief and that as far as ones religious belief is concerned man is answerable to the One True God alone. There is no forcing of one's beliefs upon another man and no punishment for leaving one's faith permitted or condoned under the banner of Islam. In such matters of faith God is the only judge.

Secularization is nothing more than destruction of the faith. When you mix blueberries in the strawberry pie does it taste the same? When you mix your own ideas into a faith the faith no longer appeals to the rights of others but just for you. There are so many sects in all faiths in the world today because there are so many people who want to have a faith all of there own just to meet their own greedy desires and control the minds of others who follow them. People want the ability to pick and choose those commandments that they are willing to follow and make those that they don't permissible. God has given Islam to all mankind not for just the needs of this or that tribe. When you infect a sterile area with your own bacteria you not only destroy the cleanliness of the area but you also infect anyone in the area with you. Only by using the pure form of the faith will it give the same results it was designed to bring about. Purity can only be kept by not infecting the area with any outside interference. This concept applies to all religion because of the sensitive and important position it holds in the life of man.

Many claim that human rights were born in Christianity. It sure is strange when authors make statements like these but offer no factual evidence. Christianity is a faith based on the idea that a man died from torture. Where is the human rights issue for him? I could see a human rights violation of a man being persecuted for his religious beliefs but is the man worth worshiping or the being he worshipped and was tortured for. You would think that even after all of this happened to their "god" that anyone of Christian faith would ever want to harm anyone through either word or sword, right? I wish I could say that is what happened but I would definitely be lying.

I will not go about proving the fact that human rights was not born in Christianity because being of African descent in this country alone is enough to prove the fact that men of Christian background committed an act that would definitely be seen as the violation of one's human rights. I am not a descendant of Americans, nor of European heritage, nor did my people migrate to the States on their own so because of some other way of life did my ancestors arrive here. I don't use the race card in my life but I will use it as an eye-opener for those blinded to the corruption that idolatry spreads.

The Qur'an teaches Muslims how to solve problems within themselves.

"...And help one another in righteousness and piety, and help not one another in sin and aggression, and keep your duty to Allah. Surely Allah is severe in requiting." (5:2).

The principle code of righteousness is laid down here as a must when dealing with others, Muslim or non-Muslim. Islam commands all Muslims to give equal treatment to peoples of all tribes and nations.

"And hold fast by the covenant of Allah all together and be not divided. And remember Allah's favor to you when you were enemies, then He united your hearts so by His favor you became brethren. And you were on the brink of fire, then He saved you from it. Thus Allah makes clear to you His Messages that you may be guided." (3:102).

During the times of Muhammad (saw) the term fire was used to symbolize war since the usage of fire was a signal to gather the tribes together for war. The Qur'an is to be used as a tool to stop men from fighting and to unite them. This tool of the Qur'an is definitely needed in these times to help men avoid this plague of violence and war that is with us today. If the Qur'an was used to end disagreements betweens the Muslims and non-Muslims of Arabia it can definitely be used today to solve the disputes between the Muslim countries and the non-Muslim nations of the world.

"And if two parties of the believers quarrel, make peace between them. Then if one of them does wrong to the other, fight that which does wrong, till if it return to Allah's command. Then if it returns to peace between them with justice act equitably. Surely Allah loves the equitable." (49:9).

This verse requires that Muslims are not to be indifferent when one part quarrels with another but in such cases they must bring every kind of pressure within the bounds of fairness and morality upon the party in error. It is the duty of every Muslim to maintain the unity of Islam.

These verses clearly show that it is obligatory of every Muslim to maintain peace and harmony inside the Muslim world because if this is not done how can it be proven to the non-Muslim world that Islam is the best way of living. Only by living one's faith can it be exemplified and copied. When one does not live up to his responsibilities the Holy Qur'an still stands as the pure teachings of God, and Muhammad (saw) his most perfect example. The weakness of man will never overshadow the brightness of Islam.

Men of all colors need to find the true solution to their problems. Only by determining what is truth and what is a lie will these groups be able to live in peace and come together as one. Only through finding a completely honest, logical, and realistic solution to the differences that exist in these opposing lifestyles will the Christian and Muslim worlds ever unite. A servant cannot serve two masters so one of these ways of life must be put to rest. But which one? Both of them claim to be the salvation of mankind while the other is its destruction. But which one?

The only way we will ever figure out which way is by examining the application of each faith in real life trials. Only by examining each faith's ability to stand up to real life trials will the true faith prevail. Only by examining the true teachings of each faith and determining which one will help mankind to exist during these harsh times will the banner of the true religion be raised. By careful and honest examination of each faith will you the reader be able to see which faith will help you and which will hurt you. I hope that your eyes will be enlightened to find the true way of life we all yearn for.

It is easy for a Christian writer to say Islam does not condone human rights. It is easy for a Western author to make a comment heard by mostly Western readers because he knows they will believe him just because they are from the same tribe and is only looking out for their interest. A farmer selling beef is not going to sell his steaks to a vegetarian community but in a meat-eating town where his product would be welcome. This is what happens everyday to the Western world. Everyday they are fed lie after lies and soon these lies they hear begin to soak into their brains and they begin to accept it for the truth and incorporate it into their lives.

I have written this book so that you my Western brothers and sisters can have a chance to hear the truth and discover whether to accept it or reject it. Jesus was mocked scorned, and crucified for bringing his message yet 2,000 years later he remains one of the greatest men of history. How will men look at me in 2,000 years for writing this book? Will they look at me as a man concerned of not only the rights of the West, of all men, or just some other crazy writer on a mission to screw up the world? I hope that this message of truth will open the eyes of the people of the West to find that the human rights shown in the Qur'an offers are the greatest gifts they could ever receive.

The Qur'an can also be used as an historical document because it tells the history of many tribes and nations of the earth. It tells of men who no longer exist and of groups who still roam the earth. It gives factual and archeological evidence of great kings and rulers who once governed over legions of men. It gives history but it contains thousands of prophecies that have come true and many more reveal themselves as time goes by.

It's not hard to see what the Western culture brings to the dinner table. The greatest gift the Western world brings to other societies is idolatry. The Western world knows nothing of the truth of worshiping the One True God, but has chosen to worship physical idols. The Roman gods. The Viking gods. The worship of Christ. The worship of the flag. The worship of money. The worship of White skin. These are the many levels of worship that the people of the West have been deceived to believe yet all of these will only fail them. The Western life because of its saturation of idolatry has nothing to offer its own citizens so what makes it think it has anything to offer other cultures of the globe? Would it seem logical for a man with no way to support and raise one child to commit to having another? America cannot even take care of and nourish its own what makes it think it is capable of raising another.

The same corruption, crime, and ignorance that plagues America will only leak into the new culture and condemn it to destroy itself just as it has done here in America. If we can't keep our yard clean who are we to call our neighbors dirty? That is one of the many problems of the West. We think so highly of ourselves yet when we ask others how they feel about us we receive hatred and contempt. I was once told by an employer of mine that it's not how we see ourselves that is true but what others see of you that is the true you. If the Western world would put itself in the shoes of others they would see the true face of West. Take a second and ask yourself, do you like what you see?

The One True God has given many commandments concerning relations with non-Muslims. In the Qur'an God states on numerous occasions that Muslims should avoid different types of non-Muslims. God gave this commandment to the Muslims for different reasons. Islam during the time of Muhammad was still in its early stages and so to keep it from being infected with any pagan beliefs the Muslims were to stand clear of the pagan Meccans to ensure the purity of the faith. This commandment was given because there were many hypocrites who would smile in the faces of the Muslims then stab them in the back. This command would help to keep them secure from harm both physically and spiritually.

Any command given by God is only meant to ensure the safety and security of God's followers. For man to question His commandments is only to insult His Greatness.

The job of rewarding and punishing in Islam is very defined. The role of rewarding and punishing lies in the hands of the One True God. Any man that feels it is his personal right to punish another man for a sin against God only desires to be God. What a heinous sin! Only an organized government can hand down punishment and even then the punishment is meant to fit the extremity of the crime. Outrageous acts of physical torture in the name of discipline are extremely forbidden in Islam. Only acts of physical crime such as murder, rape, and theft are to be punished by physical force and even then the Qur'an explains that the punishments for these crimes are to be dealt with extreme fairness and justice. A man trying to fulfill the role of God instead of trying to purify his community is only condemning his society to indifference, inequality, and moral corruption. Man does not posses the knowledge to judge fairly so only by following the true teachings of God will he be able to promote morality, kindness, and fair play in his society.

Islam is the divine way of life revealed by the God of the Heavens and Earth. To say that His divine teachings should be changed by a weak group of people is insulting to the Greatness of God. Should a parent bow down and obey his child? How unrealistic does that sound? Why should the Creator bow down to the created? This just goes to show you the level of ignorance these writers and leaders are in so-called modern society. These are the people you look towards for advice and knowledge yet they are only ignorant weak men with dreams of becoming gods. But one day they will only perish into nothingness. Will you allow their ignorance to be your doom also?

The unrealistic solutions they offer to get rid of the purity of Islam will only take them and anyone who is desperate enough to believe their lies farther and farther from the grace of God. If a man who played baseball all his life told you nothing but how boring basketball was could you believe him since he never took part in a game of basketball? Would you allow his lack of knowledge of the joy of basketball keep you away from experiencing the fun of playing basketball? You must not allow yourself to be blinded from the truth by those who are so far lost that their only goal is to take others down with them.

Their anger against the beauty of Islam exists because they know that through Islam they will loose the so-called "power" to influence and control the minds and actions of others. Now where is the freedom there? Who do you think has the greater power to influence the minds of men, men or God? Who do you think has the power to really reward or punish, men or God? Who is the Creator and who was created?

Many ignorant writers often accuse the Arabs of using terrorism as a means of restoring Islam to its original purity. The desire is not to restore the purity of Islam but to restore the strength of the Arab world. The Arab world has fallen to shreds and their desire is only to restore the physical might of the Arabs. But what they don't realize is that strength does not lie in using democracy, military, or financial power but in giving the respect back to God that He deserves. Islam has existed in the Middle East for centuries so the leaders use the tool of power and the people's ignorance of their own religion to hypnotize their people to perform acts for their personal gain just as in the Western world where Christianity has fueled many immoral acts.

By misinterpreting verses to unknowledgeable people, the leaders were free to commit immoral acts against God and man. That is how the Arab world has fallen into the situation they are in now. Islam will always exist in its pure form. The time will always come when the truth is revealed and only those who follow the right path will be able to endure the hardships they face. Their desire to bring Islam to power is false because Islam has never lost its power; it is only the light of their own people that has faded. This happens to all people except the true followers of Muhammad (saw).

SCIENCE AND EDUCATION

The Arab empire grew under the faith of Islam because God had promised the Arabs a great empire as a reward for enduring the hardships they faced in their early days and the steadfastness they showed in the face of pagan adversity. Why is it then when one group succeeds, the other groups exhibit jealousy and hate? Man without morality is no better than a pack of hyenas fighting over the dead carcass of an antelope. For men who claim to be so civilized they exhibit the same qualities of animals of the jungle. Islam is a way of life that guarantees its followers the highest of rewards in the next life as well as in this life. God is quick to reward and slow to punish all men.

Anti-Islamic writers and leaders often try to persuade others that Islam holds no joy. But what is joy? To some it is happiness, peace, comfort, or safety. But can one find complete joy in a physical object or a lie? Objects that will one day whither away, die, decay, or be proven false. The only object that will remain forever is God so to find true joy is to find joy in the One True God.

This is Islam: The complete submission of oneself to the will of God. To know that you are totally engrossed in the will and protection of the Creator of the Heavens and Earth is the purpose of all men. To know that the things you do are only for the approval of the Creator of all life. To know that your safety is provided by the All Powerful and that your needs are guaranteed to be cared for by the Bestower of All. This is true joy. Physical needs can be taken away at the drop of a dime, but it is the spiritual needs that will give you all you could possibly desire.

Early Muslim scientists studied all forms of science for the benefit of all men and have developed far too many things to discuss here. Muslim mathematicians are accredited with recognition of the concept of zero without which many other concepts could not be described or expounded upon. All science is related one way or another. All math and science it is based on principles discussed by those who came before of many different faiths and backgrounds. Just as their findings are used as a basis for those after them. Only by working together will mankind be able to unlock the mysteries of nature and science that God wills us to understand. It does not matter who found what first because the reality is that God was the first and He alone will be the last.

Science is true no matter what religion the scientist practices. What man can say that he holds the knowledge of science in his pocket? The information of science is merely the transfer of information from a higher mind to a lower mind. Man being the lower mind only receives data from God a higher source for purposes unknown by man at that time. Science is data based on facts proven to be true so it does not matter what religion the scientist is a truth will always be a truth. No matter if it is night or day the truth will remain the same. This is the beauty of Islam. Its truths and commandments all coincide with the laws of science proving all its tenants to be 100% true.

Islam does not go against any of the laws of nature or physics; it only enforces their truths. Islam is the perfect moral counterpart to the ever-revealing scientific world God has placed in nature around us. As mankind is blessed more and more with God's grace we will be able to bridge the gap between science and religion thus proving all the miracles God wishes for us to understand as merely revealed scientific knowledge at that time.

Islam agrees with and backs up all the revealed religions in their purest and truest form. The scientific evidence in the Qur'an clearly shows that the laws of faith must also follow the guidelines of nature set by the Almighty. God has given mankind the knowledge to understand the hidden secrets He has created as a way for man to ultimately discover the best way of life to live. This way is Islam. God has given us this knowledge of science to back up all the information he has revealed in His book, the Holy Qur'an. In the Qur'an God foretold the finding of the power contained in the atom and just recently this prophecy came true with the making of the atomic bomb. Many of the scientific discoveries that have been made in the last 1,500 years have been foretold in the Qur'an many years ago.

What man in the deserts of Arabia could have known of these great scientific discoveries whether they related to the past or the present? Just because God told of the finding of these great scientific discoveries He didn't say who would discover them. Just as the blessing of Islam was given to all men God also gives all men scientific knowledge. God gives us this knowledge so that we can recognize how great the knowledge, wisdom, and power God possesses. By recognizing His unlimited power and wisdom we have no choice but to submit to His will. This is Islam. The more discoveries we make the more we come to seeing His existence and greatness. This truth of His existence will only force us to accept His glory and to bow down to His Majesty. That is why here in the West our minds are kept off the thought of praising God because it will only lead us to worshiping Him and doing the righteous things we are instructed to do.

Trying to explain the existence of man has always been a topic for philosophers. God explains to man his role in the universe and teaches him how to live his life to the fullest. Doesn't this way sound better and more rewarding? Is man knowledgeable of all things or is God? Is man perfect or is God? Is man the creator of the universe or is God? Only when man stops thinking he is the almighty and gives God back His due respect will he find his way out of this maze of deception he has put himself in. It's one thing to try to learn and understand religion, but to try to think that you can better yourself without religion is a waste of time. The people of the West after separating the power of the church from the state has only drawn themselves another step away from morality and righteousness by putting power in the hands of men who base the idea of right and wrong on quotas and financial gains.

The purpose of the Qur'an is quite clear. Every team uses a playbook to implement a winning plan to bring about its success on the field of play. By executing these plays correctly the team can attempt to achieve a victory. By wandering around aimlessly you can never reach your goals. Life is exactly the same. A plan must be laid out so that success can be achieved. The Qur'an is the playbook that has been given to us by the Supreme Being that if used correctly all mankind can achieve victory in this world as well as the next. The Qur'an not only tells us what plays to execute to bring about success, but also tells us what plays were used by others before us that failed in order that we not use them. This book is very simple to use. It requires only one characteristic for its usage. The reader of the book must only be a righteous person to be able to prosper from the plan it lays forth in those mere 114 chapters.

The pursuit of education is held in the highest regards in the faith of Islam. It is only through education of science, nature, and history can man find his way out of darkness and ignorance. God in the Qur'an gives man the command to seek knowledge again and again.

"Read in the name of thy Lord who creates-Creates man from a clot of clay, Read and thy Lord is most Generous. Who taught by the pen, Taught man what he knew not." (96:1-5).

"Then they found one of Our servants whom We had granted mercy from Us and whom We had taught knowledge from Ourselves. Moses said to him; May I follow thee that thou mayest teach me of the good thou hast been taught?" (18:65,66).

"He grants wisdom to whom He pleases. And whoever is granted wisdom, he indeed is given a great good. And none mind but men of understanding." (2:269).

While faith brings about the spiritual and moral development of man, knowledge brings about his intellectual development, and therefore stands next in importance to faith. The first revelations that came to the Holy Prophet (saw) concerned the education of man. These verses not only lay stress on both reading and writing but also speak of the Lord of Honor in this connection. The Holy Qur'an directs the Muslim to seek more and more knowledge. God constantly refers to knowledge as wealth. The Holy Prophet (saw) made it very important for his followers past and present to seek knowledge of all forms. The Prophet (saw) desired even that those who were considered to be the lowest in society to be uplifted to the highest level through education. Islam lays the basis of mass education of all men, women, and children. Islam makes learning compulsory for all Muslims. A warning is given that when a nation gives up on the acquisition of knowledge, its downfall is sure. The Holy Prophet (saw) is reported to have said:

"Go back to your people and teach them."

"Let him who is present impart knowledge to him who is absent."

"The seeking of knowledge is obligatory upon every Muslim."

The proclamation by the Qur'an that Muhammad (saw) is a universal Prophet with a universal message is in itself tantamount to declaring that the religion of Islam is founded on rationality. No religion with any element of irrationality can be acceptable to the universal conscience of man. The Qur'an manifestly acknowledges the role of rationality for the attainment of truth without drawing any separating lines between religious or secular truths. Truth is the religion of Islam and Islam is the religion of Truth. Islam requires no compulsion for the transmission of its message, the only instrument it needs is rationality. As such, Islam invokes human intellect to investigate the truth of the Qur'anic teachings with reference to the study of human nature, history, and rationality.

"And the Jews say: The hand of Allah is tied up. Their own hands are shackled and they are cursed for what they say. Nay both His hands are spread out. He disburses as He pleases. And that which has been revealed to thee from thy Lord will certainly make many of them increase in inordinacy and disbelief. And We have cast among them enmity and hatred until the day of resurrection. Whenever they kindle a fire for war Allah puts it out, and they strive to make mischief in the land. And Allah loves not the mischief makers." (5:64).

The early Muslims of Arabia were mostly poor people. When they left Mecca they had left most of their belongings. Many of the Arab Muslims were an agriculture community and naturally not rich. Other races of people had on the other hand carried on business and carried on dealings with very high interest. These people constantly taunted the poor Muslims saying that Allah hands were tied. The words *"both His hands are spread out"* indicates that God will enrich the Muslims. The blessing of God came in the form of a black syrup like liquid that has sprung from the ground of all the Arab lands giving the Arabs wealth beyond their wildest dreams; yes, I refer to oil. Could this prophecy be fulfilled any more completely?

The prosperity of the Western nations has been given to them for a reason. It has been given to them to show the ever-encompassing mercy of God. Even after all the wrongdoings committed by the West God has given them the chance to repent and change their ways. He gives them the opportunity at the dawn of each day to change their ways and turn to the path of righteousness He has laid out for all humanity. Yet the misguidance of the Western man continues to overpower their need of seeking righteousness. Everyday God allows the sun to continue to rise over the lands of the West yet they still haven't gotten the picture. They continue to gloat over their achievements and their false sense of power. They continue to give no thanks or praise to the One who deserves all praise. What have they really achieved? Have their puny creations come anywhere near the infinite wisdom and knowledge of God, the All-Knowing. Has their knowledge of the universe come any where near the knowledge of the Creator of the Universe? I cannot even comprehend a number small enough to say what percentage of knowledge man has attained compared to the One True God. Just because they have made a god of a man they think they possess the same power of the One True God. The praise of their false power only leads them farther away from the greatness of the One True God.

Don't pat yourself on the back thinking the game is over and the West has won because as long as you are straying farther from the One True God the fourth quarter will only lead you to the end of your winning streak and you know the old saying, "The higher you go, the harder the fall." The only thing that is going to prevent that fall, again, is to return to the right path. No amount of technological advances, military might, or financial greatness will be able to stop the wrath of God. Wrath, now that is a strong word especially when it pertains to the Creator of the Heavens and Earth. Forget comparing the physical strength of the West to that of other nations do we have what it takes to stop the punishment of God? Do we have the power to stop floods, tornadoes, or lightning?

Other nations before us thought they had the power to resist the punishment of God, but today they are nowhere to be found. What makes you think you can today? Only through the path righteousness can His wrath be avoided. Islam is that path of righteousness.

We think it is all about the haves and the have-nots but what is there to have? Physical power. What is physical power? It is the lie that you are all-powerful. Since God is All-Powerful why is man jealous of God? Men lying to themselves and others saying that they are gods. The men of the West believe they have the most powerful armies, amassed the greatest fortunes, and politically control the fate of the world, but what a joke. Would any army the West possesses be able to stand a second of the power of God? Would all the money in the world buy them a way out of God's wrath? Would the power of any politician help him escape God's scorn?

And then there is the men of the East who dream of that same false power. The physical power they illusion the West to posses has blinded them into dreaming that that same power is due to them. It's a catch up game with the West for seeing who can be more disobedient to the commandments of God. Everybody is jealous of God and instead of trying to submit to His will they are trying to test it. What insanity! Neither side is jealous of each other but of God himself and the power He alone possesses. Whatever power man thinks he possesses will not help in this life or the next. If God wanted to, He could end our lives now and what could we do about it? Yet men continue to believe that they are not going to die.

FRIEND OR FOE?

The Qur'an gives guidance to the Muslims and also explains how to deal with those who haven't yet experienced the beauty of the Islamic way of life. The Qur'an is very explicit as to how the Muslims are to deal with the different types of non-Muslims.

"Allah forbids you not respecting those who fight you not for religion, nor drive you forth from your homes, that you show them kindness and deal with them justly. Surely Allah loves the doers of justice." (60:8).

This verse was revealed at a time when the relations between the Muslims and the disbelievers were difficult due to the continuous state of war between the two groups. This verse clearly states that Muslims are allowed to engage in friendly relations with non-Muslims as long as the non-Muslims are not engaged with the fore mentioned activities. This was a warning that if engaging in relations with the enemy who they are in combat with at that time would bring about destruction on the part of the Muslims both physically during battle and spiritually since the religion of Islam was still in its early stages. This verse was revealed because the Muslims needed to remain firm in their beliefs.

Even the Holy Prophet (saw) was quoted as saying concerning the disbelievers. Usahmah ibn Zaid relates that the Holy Prophet (saw) passed by a company of people which comprised of Muslims, idol worshippers, and Jews, and he greeted them with the salutation of peace (Buhkari and Muslim). This story clearly states how the Prophet felt about non-Muslims. He felt nothing but love and compassion for his fellow man no matter the faith or way of life he professed.

"Fight those who believe not in Allah, nor in the Last Day, nor forbid that which Allah and His messenger have forbidden, nor follow the Religion of Truth, out of those who have been given the Book, until they pay the tax in acknowledgement of superiority and they are in a state of subjection." (9:29).

Though other groups of people for a long time assisted the idolatrous Arabians in their struggle to uproot Islam the great Christian power, the Roman Empire, had only just mobilized its forces to force the subjection of the new religion. As the object of the Christian Empire was simply the subjection of the Muslims, the words in their final vanquishment are different from those dealing with the final vanquishment of the idolatrous Arabians. The Qur'an neither required that the non-Muslims accept Islam nor was it in any way its object to bring the Christians under Arab rule.

The Christians attempted to take the Muslims over through the use of the sword resulting in utter loss. The non-Muslims were ordered to pay a tax that was taken by every non-Muslim citizen. Whereby they ratify the pact that ensures them protection because it is a compensation for the protection that is guaranteed them, thus freeing them from military service. This tax allowed non-Muslims to be able to live comfortably and freely under the protection of the Muslims.

We here in the West pay taxes on a regular basis in order to ensure our government and military is well provided for to protect our country from aggression. Muhammad (saw) simply enforced a tax to the non-Muslims who wished to live under the protection of the Muslims without having to fight. This tax more or less made the Muslims hired bodyguards to protect their non-Muslim counterparts. The Muslims also paid taxes that helped pay for the everyday needs of the running of society and the helping of the poor. The non-Muslims were not being singled out they were just doing their part to ensure the safety of the society they lived in. The Prophet's (saw) noble and moral character did not allow him to over charge or cheat the non-Muslims out of their money or property.

The greed of a man is inspired by his lower demons, never from God. If a chef messes up the meal because he chose to not follow the recipe is it his fault or fault of the recipe? God has given mankind the perfect recipe for living on earth. If man has allowed himself to be distracted by the greed of the physical world should God be the one to blame? To say that God gave the wrong instructions would say God is not perfect. That is mere insanity. Men are stubborn and only by following the correct guidance correctly will they prosper. Would the greed of a Christian be blamed on Christianity? Would you punish the pig for the fox stealing your chicken?

Western authors like to say how human rights filtered from the West, yet I see no proof that human rights ever existed in the West. Have we here in the West caught amnesia or have we chosen to forget the history of the Western nations? Have we all been bought off by pride to look away at the mention of our history? The United States claims to be a place of human rights but when did this happen? Can any historian dare to give an exact date when human rights took precedence over greed in the U.S.? Has the truth of the founding of this nation been totally deleted by the minds of its citizens? This is why America will not find peace. It was rotten at its core and only through a totally opposite frame of mind will it ever survive this storm.

We must be honest with ourselves; the United States was created for White people. This land was never meant to be the home of people of color unless they were slaves. The human rights declared by this government were only meant for White males. You might say I might be being a little hard on Caucasian men but did you ever think that White slave owners in their wildest dreams could imagine their daughter sitting next to a black boy in school? We act like slavery was an ancient thing but it was abolished less than 200 years ago. When did human rights filter in? People in America need to realize that living a lifestyle is more than just talking about it; their actions must also convey the message they follow.

Conquests of the Romans are looked upon with greatness, yet when the Arabs expanded their empire we frown with contempt. The Romans were White people so it is only common sense that White people would be proud of the might of their ancestors. But is pride a good thing? Would you a White person be just as proud of the Roman conquests if you were born African? That's the problem with people we only care about ourselves and not of others. If we could become another color and walk in another race's or sex's shoes I'm sure we would see the world differently. We would definitely think more of others feelings.

The Caesars, Genghis Khan, Hannibal, and Napoleon all at one point in time conquered nearly ¾ of Africa, Asia, and Europe all through the use of the sword, spear, or arrow. All of these emperors are praised for their military tactfulness, never-ending ferocity, and strength in battle. Sounds like praise and admiration for their tenacity in the field of war. On the other hand when the Arabs began to sweep across into Europe and Asia their conquests in battle aren't as glamorized as the battles of Julius Caesar. Why?

To praise one warrior means to praise them all. Why is it that when the Arabs conquered territories it was called the Islamic empire but no one ever called the Roman Empire the Pagan Empire or the Christian empire? This comes from the fact that it was not the people whom the European leaders felt truly threatened by but it was the conquerors way of life that threatened them. What about Islam makes them quiver with fear?

Empires fall but religions last for centuries and if all of Europe would accept Islam the power of the Christian Church would be destroyed forever. The Church knew that the Arab Empire would not last forever just as other empires before. In order to keep the European people from accepting Islam they made the faith of Islam the ultimate enemy rather than just the Arab invaders. The leaders of today have chosen to resume this battle against Islam. Thus killing two birds with one stone Arab and Islam were fused together to mean the same thing thus giving Western people a physical face to hate matching the ideology.

Many Western authors use the term "House of Islam." The term "House" is a literary trick. Let me explain. If you have a house it has walls and a roof. No matter how big or small. Whether it is a one-room shack or a four-acre mansion it still consists of mere walls and a roof. It also might have windows. Windows so its inhabitants can use to look out or maybe for outsiders to look in. This house needs a door for those inside to leave or maybe for outsiders to come in. There's that 'o' word again. The purpose of the walls is to divide and separate the conditions on the outside from affecting the conditions on the inside or vice versa. The term "House of Islam" is used to separate the Muslim world from the outsiders. Who are the outsiders? White People. The purpose of putting Islam behind walls is to keep it from being seen by White people here in America. You. Why would someone paint the picture that Islam is not for Western people when it is only a way of life designed to ensure peace and prosperity to all nations including Western nations? Don't White people deserve peace and freedom also? You must tear down the walls of ignorance and see for yourself what peace and prosperity awaits you within Islam.

So many Western authors often use words like "confine" and "enclose" to try to give their readers the impression that Islam is a prison-like faith. They use these words to make their readers feel that Islam is a faith that causes its followers to be held back or held against their will. These Western authors couldn't be any farther from the truth. Islam sets you free. It is a faith that helps man reach his ultimate potential through the usage of morality, common sense, and closeness to God. The only thing Islam imprisons in man is the desire to commit wrongdoings. By following the commandments of God one becomes a better person making the world they live in a better and safer place. Would this sound like a place you want to live in? Islam can get you there. I promise.

It's easy to point the finger at other countries and their treatment of minorities but what would happen if we got a time machine and traveled back about 250 years and looked at the history of the Western man's treatment of minorities on these shores. Let's go:

1. Native Americans—millions killed in the theft of North America

2. Africans—who knows how many kidnapped, enslaved, murdered during Slavery

3. Women-property of their husbands/fathers, no social or political rights

4.   Dropping of the atomic bomb, twice killing over two hundred thousand civillians

Now we can all sit here and say well these things don't exist now and I would have to agree, but do you think that just because we have chosen to forget these events that makes them not true and that they don't have any affect on us today? Are we that blind or just arrogant? Do we really think that by forgetting our wrongdoings that makes us makes us perfect in the eyes of the world? Do you think other countries of the world have forgotten the atrocities committed by the West under the banner of idolatry? Do you think that in forgetting the wrongdoings that were perpetrated here in our country we also have forgotten which religious belief the perpetrators of these harmful deeds practiced? We have gotten rid of these acts of harm, but why does the way of life that allowed these acts still exist?

The Qur'an does not forget to give guidance about dealing with Christians:

"...and thou wilt find the nearest in friendship to the believers to be those who say, We are Christians. That is because there are priests and monks among them and because they are not proud." (5:82).

The Christians are nearer to Islam than other ways of life because there are still many among them who fear and worship God in humility. Christianity at its core also teaches humbleness and goodness which are also found in the teachings of Islam. Nowhere in the Qur'an does God instruct anyone to inflict harm on another person just because of difference in belief. The Christian people of the West need to understand that the closer they search for truth the closer they will get to Islam, the ultimate worship of God. It is only the time they waste in this transition the longer they must suffer for their misguidance. God has given them Islam that they may free themselves from the pains they suffer today.

The Qur'an was revealed to enhance the spiritual and moral development of mankind. Has mankind changed that much over the last 1,500 years? Has the accepted notions of right and wrong changed over the last 1,500 years? Only by using the information delivered to its complete accuracy will mankind be able to understand the usefulness of this great tool. When cooking an item if you have the correct measurements of ingredients, but combine them out of order or don't use all the ingredients your meal will not fulfill the desired taste you wished to acquire. The Qur'an is a tool that all the ingredients inside must be used and combined in the appropriate order set by God. Any ingredients taken out or added to this divine recipe will only cause the user of the recipe to fail to meet the expectations desired by God.

THE SOLUTION

Islam is not a threat to the West. I can say that because I am a Westerner. A threat is something that causes harm. Islam can only improve the life of someone and his society. Whether in the East or the West Islam is the only cure for the problems of mankind. A pure piece of meat can give the body the proper nutrients it needs but the same piece of meat when infected with bacteria will cause the body to get sick and even die. The pure Islam will only give the West the nutrients and vitamins it yearns to attain. Islam is the reason thousands upon thousands of Europeans poor and rich came to the shores of North America. They thought that by migrating to a new country they could find freedom through economic salvation yet the real freedom they were looking for was freedom of the heart and mind, not just the wallet. The search for financial wealth only enslaved the masses to the inner greed that lies inside the hearts of all men. Only by suppressing this demon will man free himself from this invisible enslaver. Islam is the pathway to the final free world where men of all colors wish to migrate.

The mistakes we have made in the past can only help us learn a valuable lesson for the future yet today the leaders of the Western world continue to make the same mistakes over and over. To say something is modern is very vague because of the quickness of time. Phonographs were once said to be very modern, then came the revolutionary 8-track, but now we have compact discs and mp3 players and who knows what other invention is right around the corner. Morality also evolves as man continues to attempt to solve the many social and political problems the world faces everyday. All of these problems were solved 1,500 years ago when Islam was given to mankind. All the problems that man will ever face was given a remedy by God in the form of the Qur'an. As man continues to search for the solution he will continue to realize that the answers to all of his problems were right in front of his face yet he chose to beat around the bush and cling to his old and useless ways.

There is only one voice of Islam. He is not I. He is not the thousands of so-called Islamic scholars. The one and only voice of Islam is the One True God. Only the word of God can speak for Islam and offer the true meaning of the faith. When a European man commits an act in the name of Christ that is deemed immoral by general society do we condemn Christianity as a whole? What would make him the official voice of Christianity? Should a way of life be condemned because of one man's actions? If the answer is yes than how has any religion withstood the test of time when so many men from every faith have committed enormous atrocities in the name of their faiths?

A Muslim submits only to the will of God. If you submit to God whom do you have to fear? A true Muslim has no enemies because an enemy can inflict harm upon you but if the One True God is on your side what can harm you. The true meaning of submission is the firmest belief that God protects you at all times no matter the situation. By fearing no one but God a true believer gives in to no lower desires or threats no matter if it is a threat from inside himself or outside. It is incorrect to say that the Muslim world is struggling. It is the Arab world that is struggling because their belief in God has weakened and so they are forced to struggle with the problems and threats of this physical world instead of allowing God to protect and guide them.

Islam is the water that helps the tree of mankind to grow. If the water becomes contaminated it looses its strength to give life. The True Islam is the distilled water of the world. All the contaminated forms of this faith will only cause their followers to be weakened, sickened, and ultimately disappear. Only in its True pure form will Islam be able to deliver man to the level of moral upliftment it was given for almost 2,000 years ago. Used in its proper formula, the original recipe will give the same blessings it gave to the pagan Meccans resulting in an assurgency of truth, freedom, and blessings. This same moral and spiritual rebirth is what the West is looking for. Look no further, the truth of Islam is here for you.

Muslims do not have to assimilate in any country whether Capitalist or Socialist because the moral code that a Muslim lives by allows him to thrive and contribute to the complete betterment of the society. The moral codes of Islam are the basic moral codes built into humans at birth. Islam is the only religion that claims to cater to all the basic human instincts and teaches us how to regulate and control all immoral and moral desires that all men have. Islam teaches a Muslim how to exist alongside non-Muslims or in any type of environment. The moral code set by Islam is a barrier to all outside influences, political shortcomings, and financial barriers. It makes the Muslim the sole bearer of the responsibility of maintaining his own conduct within himself, his family, his country, and the world. The real assimilation that the West wants is for Muslims to give up Islam all together. This will not happen. That is like learning how to ride a bike then after 10 years of riding the rider would go back to using training wheels. Wouldn't happen.

What gives the West the right to define peace? The world is divided into so many races that we have forgotten that we all are one family. Islam is here to remind us. Being that we are one family the concept of peace can only be gained when all members of the family are happy. It is not peace when one third of the world is eating and the other two are starving. It is not peace when one third of the world is content and the other two are under the sword. Peace will not be obtained until all mankind is on the same moral path treating the other as he would like himself to be treated.

Only when every man learns to resist his lower animal instincts of greed, lust, and hatred will the possibility of peace begin to exist on earth. God says that the best of men are the most righteous and that the final judge of mankind is God Himself. We must all examine ourselves honestly to see if we are living up to God's expectations of righteousness with our fellow man, whether he is of the same color or not.

A sect is an offshoot of one perfect belief. Do not waste your time and energy on the many branches go right to the trunk. The source. The beginning. Only at the base of this belief will you find the true meaning of Islam. Only by examining the base of Islam will you be able to answer this question for yourself. A base that still thrives in the minds and actions of over ten millions Muslims worldwide.

The One True God created all religions, but Islam is the most perfect. In Islam the main belief is the existence of One God. If this same God existed forever and is responsible for the deliverance of revelation to all the known accepted prophets then this One God would have delivered the same message to all these prophets. It would be totally illogical for this One God to reveal different groups of men different messages. This One True God would want to see all of the men he created living in peace so He would reveal the same message to all the different tribes of mankind in order to unite them in brotherhood.

The Western public is very misguided about Islam and has not been given the true meaning of Islam. It has received so much incorrect information that they have no idea of the beauty of Islam. True Islam is the dream the Western man has been searching for made into reality. Only by getting the correct information about Islam will they realize that this is the truth they have been searching for centuries. True Islam is the American dream. But instead of sleeping, the Western man will be wide-awake to see the plant of Islam deliver the fruits for which they yearn.

The difference between the Bible and the Qur'an is that one book was meant for one group of people during one time while the other book was meant for all mankind till the end of time. That second book was meant for you Western people. A young boy cannot fit a grown man's pants while at the same time a grown man cannot fit a small child's pants. The Bible is the small boy's pants trying to be worn by the grown man of today's world. The Bible only offers the teachings that were only meant to be worn by the young boy of two thousand years ago.

Science has proven that mankind has evolved over the centuries physically so of course he must evolve mentally. Mankind has evolved mentally and morally so only a teaching that is able to correspond with the changes of man is suitable to fit his needs today. As mankind's mind evolves so do the tendencies to stray from the right path. In order to combat these growing problems a guidebook must be given to handle all the problems that mankind will ever face. The guidebook must be able to offer a reasonable and practical solution to all the problems man will encounter. The guidebook must be able to have guidelines that are applicable towards the survival and physical protection of mankind as a whole.

Islam and Christianity shape different personalities. If you dug into the ground would you reach the sky? No matter how far you dug would you reach the sky? The question is, what faith is going to give you the results that will benefit you? Islam and Christianity are two different ways of life. Both ways of life teach and install different ideologies in the practitioner. Both ways of life teach different ways of behavior and different methods of dealing with the vast situations that occur in ones life. Both ways of life regulate the actions and thoughts of the follower in different ways. But the question you must ask still remains the same. Which way of life is giving you the results you are looking for? Are you still experiencing the same problems over and over? Is your faith giving you the information to tackle the many problems you face in your daily lives?

Only by solving the problems you face can you acknowledge the validity of your way of life. That is the difference between Islam and Christianity. Islam shows mankind how to solve the problem before it arises while Christianity tells what to do after the wrongdoing is committed. But after the action is committed can it be taken back? Will this action cause a wave of other actions to take place also? Is it not better to not commit the first action at all? Throughout the history of the Western world the usage of violence has been a tool to achieve power in every aspect of Western life. Whether it is the biggest bank account or the largest gun, achieving power is the ultimate goal. Even spirituality is a tool used by those in charge to control the thoughts of its people. Would they rather have their citizens practice a faith that teaches them to accept a lie or a religion that teaches the truth about every aspect of life? Would they rather utilize a religion that teaches separatism or a faith that teaches all men are created equal?

The Western nations try to build up the pride of their citizens to the point that they care not of the burdens and problems of other nations. Through the separation of the church and state, the church has lost all the power they used to have and thus the state has been given the ability to mold its citizens according to what it wants to be right and wrong. The U.S. is a capitalist nation that believes in the gain of the dollar bill instead of believing in the One True God. Without the correct knowledge, Christianity offers no solutions to the problems the West faces. If you went to your family doctor for diagnosis on a backache but he found nothing to cure the problem what would you do? Go see another doctor. That is what Islam is. Islam is the other doctor whom the Western world must sooner or later see after it has exhausted all the effort of its less knowledgeable family doctor. Once the West begins to see the wonderful insight Islam offers to the problems faced in the West they will run into the office of Islam.

The question is how long will the West allow itself to suffer under the misguidance and the lies of their leaders? The same leaders who continue to allow the message of violence and hatred to pour into our homes, schools, and workplaces. Only the complete true code of Islam holds the keys to lock all the doors of violence that are wide open in the Western society.

Is high morality worth changing in anyone? When one reaches a stage of evolution that does nothing but increase the amount of ones high moral being is it worth changing? Islam is that high moral code and the highest form of man's evolution. We think of evolution as something physical, but it is the spiritual and moral evolution of man that will change him in the years to come. Islam raises the bar set by any moral code. Islam is the perfect moral code for the upliftment of mankind. It is the ultimate medicine for the social ailments of civilization. If you were sick would you want the complete medicine or just enough to cure you half way?

The only thing the West can prepare itself for is the acceptance of the true Islam. The Western nations will accept the truth of Islam or they will suffer the same consequences nations before them have suffered. These same plagues that were sent against many other nations have also been sent against the West, yet they choose not to recognize the signs. It is not the threat of destruction from other nations but it is the inner evils of man's lower self that infect the masses of the Western world. It is the inner evils that are hidden deep in the minds and the cultures of the Western world. It is not that the West must become like the East because they have also strayed from their pure teachings. They must become righteous to avoid the disaster they are so quickly approaching. Only through righteousness will they avoid the inevitable. Islam is the only code of living that will enable the Western race to survive the test of life.

Islam means submission to the will of God. This simple yet powerful statement provides man with the complete way of living. This simple life is the ultimate form of human evolution. It is the last stage of mankind, as we know today. This is the lifestyle that man has dreamed of finding. Through trials and errors this is what mankind has been searching for. Islam is the final destiny of the people of the West. My Western brothers and sisters this is your final frontier. This is the dream you have been searching for and the freedom from persecution you have been running to. This is the joy you yearn for everyday. This is the solution to all the problems you face in yourselves, your families, your country, and the world. No one can force you to pick up this banner of freedom, but I can tell you that the longer you wait the worse the situation will get for you. The more people that are uneducated, the more people will die in wars based on ignorance and greed. You think that you can overcome these problems you face without the truth but you can't. You think that your government will save you from these vicious perils, they won't. You think Christianity will save you. I regret to tell you Jesus Christ is never coming back. The longer you wait for his return the longer you will suffer. The solution is here. It is waiting to free you. All you must do is reach out and look for it. Islam is the only way out of the madness you are blinded by today. Islam is the only way to free your children from the evils they are surrounded by. The choice is yours to accept or reject but the time is flying by. The choice is yours. Freedom awaits you.

"*In the name of Allah the Gracious the Merciful.*
By the fleeting time!—
Surely man is in a state of loss,
Except those who believe and do good works, and exhort one another to the Truth,
and exhort one another to patience." (103:1-3).

Wajid@prodigy.net

978-0-595-35143-5
0-595-35143-3

www.ingramcontent.com/pod-product-compliance
Lightning Source LLC
Chambersburg PA
CBHW030347290526
45785CB00004B/1630